Instructor's Manual for *Human Resource and Contract Management in the Public School: A Legal Perspective*

Instructor's Manual for *Human Resource and Contract Management in the Public School: A Legal Perspective*

Bernadette Marczely
David W. Marczely

A SCARECROWEDUCATION BOOK

The Scarecrow Press, Inc.
Lanham, Maryland, and Oxford
2003

A SCARECROWEDUCATION BOOK

Published in the United States of America
by Scarecrow Press, Inc.
A Member of the Rowman & Littlefield Publishing Group
4720 Boston Way, Lanham, Maryland 20706
www.scarecroweducation.com

PO Box 317
Oxford
OX2 9RU, UK

ISBN 0-8108-4603-0 (pbk: alk. paper) ISBN: 978-0-8108-4603-6

∞™ The paper used in this publication meets the minimum requirements of American National Standard for Information Sciences—Permanence of Paper for Printed Library Materials, ANSI/NISO Z39.48-1992.
Manufactured in the United States of America.

Contents

How to Use This Instructor's Manual

This instructor's manual has been designed to complement the text by providing instructors with an introductory summary of each chapter's Pivotal Concepts, essentially an outline of chapter content and a guide for instruction. This chapter summary and outline can be used to plan lectures, activities, and assignments.

The concept outline for each chapter will be followed by Suggestions for Classroom Discussion, Research, and Activities. This section is designed to link human resource management theory to the reality of actual implementation. That is, students will be asked to discuss the ways in which their school districts address the human resource problems presented in each chapter, and to evaluate the effectiveness of these procedures in light of the chapter's concepts and concerns.

In addition, the manual provides sample Test Questions and Answers that instructors may use to measure student understanding of the concepts presented in each chapter. These test questions and answers are, for the most part, taken directly from the text and highlight the central concepts to be learned. Ideally, the instructor's manual and text should be used together for optimum learning.

Chapter One

Human Resource and Contract Management in the Public School: A Legal Perspective

PIVOTAL CONCEPTS

In an effort to define human resource and contract management, this chapter looks at the factors that directly affect human resource and contract management.

Concept 1

Employees are every organization's most vital resources, and research has shown that employee needs must be addressed before the organizational mission can be met. These needs may be real and/or psychological, and have been described as having both hierarchical and maintenance roles in determining how employees perform. Human resource management in education attempts to create an employment environment that is fair, impartial, and predictable through bureaucratic management, an approach often at odds with fostering the intrinsic catalysts for achievement identified in human resource management research.

Concept 2

The public school human resource manager is best identified by the many and varied responsibilities of the position. In light of this wide range of responsibility, one or more administrative positions within a school system can define its human resource management system. However, all administrators engaged in human resource management must have an understanding of how law, finance, collective bargaining, and policy interact in the school environment. Human resource managers may be line or staff employees, that is, they may function as decision makers or informational resources.

Concept 3

Human resource management is directly affected by national, state and local laws, regulations, and policies. School districts will reflect the goals and resources of their constituents, determining such factors as class size and staffing as well as local responses to state and federally mandated policies and procedures.

Concept 4

In recent years, Congress has passed a plethora of laws that directly affect human resource management. These federal laws, together with constitutionally protected rights, cannot be overruled by either state laws or collectively bargained agreements. State laws and local contracts can give more protections in the workplace, but they cannot give fewer protections than those provided by the Constitution and federal laws.

Concept 5

Human resource management will also be affected by national politics and political trends regarding such educational issues as accountability and teacher testing, certification, and tenure. Federal funding for education is often tied to compliance with the politically popular federal legislation affecting the workplace.

Concept 6

States are directly responsible for public education. Thus, state constitutions, laws, regulations, and policies have an even more direct effect on human resource management. State laws may simply reflect federal laws, or they may enhance employee federal rights. Employees who feel their workplace rights have been violated may sue in either state or federal courts.

Concept 7

State boards of education are directly responsible for each state's educational program, promulgating rules and regulations to implement state legislation addressing educational and employment issues in the public schools. In addition, states provide the bulk of funding for their public schools.

Concept 8

Local boards of education exert the most immediate and direct affect on human resource management, preparing and disseminating all local human resource policies and procedures. Boards are legally responsible for following state and federal laws, and for complying with their own policies and procedures. They also control local school spending, and participate, either directly or indirectly, in collective bargaining. The courts rarely substitute their own judgment for that of school boards with reasonable rules and regulations in place.

Concept 9

Local school board policy will inevitably be influenced by district history. Local school board rules, regulations, and funding reflect local concerns viewed through the lens of past local experience.

Concept 10

While not all states have laws allowing teachers to collectively bargain, in those states where teachers may bargain, the contract will control human resource management. The contract will address all issues related to wages, hours, and terms and conditions of employment, and will establish a protocol for grieving perceived violations.

Concept 11

Labor law deals with the workplace rights and responsibilities of employees protected by collectively negotiated agreements. Employment law deals with the workplace rights and responsibilities of employees who do not collectively bargain.

Concept 12

Human resource managers exercise both ministerial and discretionary powers. Ministerial power is the delegated authority to follow existing laws and policies. Discretionary power is the delegated authority to exercise personal judgment and discretion in situations not clearly defined by existing laws and policies.

SUGGESTIONS FOR CLASSROOM DISCUSSION, RESEARCH, AND ACTIVITIES

1. Have students discuss and compare their own and their classmates' school districts' successes and/or failures in addressing Maslow's hierarchy of needs as depicted in figure 1.1.

2. Have students identify the person responsible for each human resource function discussed in chapter 1 at the building level and at the district level. Who retains the ultimate ministerial and discretionary power for each function?

3. Have students interview a public school human resource manager regarding preparation for the position, i.e., educational background, experience, and certification or licensure that qualified the interviewee for this position.

4. Have students identify school employees who collectively bargain and those who do not, and compare negotiated with nonnegotiated employment contracts. Is there a tangible difference in statements regarding wages, hours, and terms and conditions of employment?

5. Have students give examples of specific federal, state, and local laws and policies at each level that directly affect some aspect or function of human resource management in the public school.

CHAPTER 1: TEST QUESTIONS AND ANSWERS

1. Describe the essential difference between Maslow's heirarchy of needs and Herzberg's hygiene factors.

Answer: The central difference between Maslow and Herzberg is that Maslow thought of every need as a potential motivator, with the range of human needs in a prepotent hierarchical order, whereas Herzberg argued that only the higher-order needs are truly motivating, with lower-order needs being simply maintenance factors.

2. How does Weber's bureacratic theory of human resource management differ from those of Maslow and Herzberg?

Answer: Weber's bureaucratic approach to human resource management is based on the theory that organizations should be impersonal, minimizing irrational personal and emotional factors in order to provide a workplace with minimum friction and confusion. There should be a division of labor based on functional specialization; a hierarchy of authority; a system of rules governing the rights and duties of employees; a system of procedures for dealing with work situations; and selection and promotion based only on technical competence.

3. What minimal course work would prepare one to function as a public school human resource manager?

Answer: Human resource managers should minimally have completed courses and training in *public school administration, school law, collective bargaining and contract management, school finance,* and *clinical supervision,* as well as a regimen of field experience as building level administrators.

4. Give an example of how the First Amendment's protection of religious freedom can have an impact on human resource management.

Answer: A human resource manager in a public school cannot ask about or consider religious affiliation in hiring school employees.

5. Give an example of a state law that affects human resource administration hiring practices.

Answer: Most states have laws requiring that teachers hired by public schools be licensed by the state, thereby assuring that they have been properly prepared for their specific assignments. (There are other viable responses to this question.)

6. In the State of Ohio public school administrators cannot collectively bargain. How then can they, and other nonunionized employees, protect their rights?

Answer: Employees who do not collectively bargain have rights and responsibilities as individuals that emanate primarily from state and federal legislation, and legal precedents set in employment law cases. They are not members of unions protected by collectively bargained agreements.

7. School administrators have both discretionary and ministerial powers. In the fact patterns that follow determine whether the administrator is being required to exercise discretionary or ministerial power, and discuss the administrator's potential vulnerability to lawsuit in each instance.

a. There is a state law requiring that all public buildings, including schools, be equipped with functioning fire alarms on every floor. The custodian in Maplewood Elementary School was ill during the first semester of the school year and the alarm system was never checked. The principal of Maplewood Elementary had also neglected conducting the mandated fire drills that would have shown that at least half of the alarms were not working.

Answer: This is an example requiring the exercise of *ministerial* power. There is a law requiring the administrator to be sure that all fire alarms are functioning. This principal can be sued because the law prescribing action was ignored.

b. Two candidates for a teaching position, one Caucasian and one African-American, apply for the position of assistant principal at Maplewood Elementary. Both candidates have virtually the same credentials, but the principal feels the Caucasian candidate's administrative style would be easier to work with and would better address the immediate needs of the school community.

Answer: There is no law in this fact pattern prescribing the hiring of one candidate over the other. When both have virtually the same credentials, the decision to hire one or the other is discretionary, and can be based on the perception of administrative style. The principal cannot be sued for making this *discretionary* decision. However, if the principal had based the decision to hire on race, in direct violation of state and federal civil rights legislation, a *ministerial duty* would have been breached and the principal could be sued.

8. As discussed in this chapter, administrative positions can be either *staff* or *line* positions. Give a brief job description of a human resource manager functioning in a *staff* position, and a brief job description for a human resource manager functioning in a *line* position.

Answer: A human resource manager functioning in a *staff* position would gather information and facts to assist building and central office administrators in developing and implementing effective administrative employment policies and practices. A human resource manager functioning in a *line* position would develop policies and procedures for all aspects of human resource management in a district, and would monitor their implementation and effectiveness.

9. List the major functions that define human resource management.

Answer: Record Keeping, Planning, Job Description Development, Recruitment, Applicant Screening, Interviewing and Selection, Hiring, Induction, Supervision, Benefit Management, Negotiations, Grievance Administration, Policy Development, Policy Evaluation, Education.

10. Describe your school district with respect to goals, resources, and population, and discuss how your school district's profile directly impacts human resource management in your district.

Answer: Responses to this question will vary.

Chapter Two

Collective Bargaining

PIVOTAL CONCEPTS

This chapter defines and discusses the role collective bargaining, where it exists, plays in human resource management. The chapter gives a brief history of bargaining and examines the political philosophies leading to either state adoption or prohibition of public sector collective bargaining, especially for teachers. Union, management, and employee rights and responsibilities in states with and without collective bargaining laws are compared from a legal perspective.

Concept 1

Collective bargaining or negotiations is a process by which groups of employees with similar backgrounds, assignments, and needs organize for the purpose of meeting with their employers and bargaining, as a group, for discussion of wages, hours, and terms and conditions of employment. The concept of negotiations is premised on the belief that there is strength in numbers.

Concept 2

The private sector labor movement began in the middle of the nineteenth century, but it wasn't until the passage of the National Labor Relations Act (NLRA), also known as the Wagner Act, in 1935, that private sector employees won the right to join unions and collectively bargain. In 1959, Wisconsin became the first state to actually pass a law mandating compulsory collective bargaining for state public employees. Connecticut, Massachusetts, and Michigan, in 1965, and Rhode Island, in 1966, were the first states to follow Wisconsin's lead in legislating mandatory compulsory collective bargaining for state public employees.

Concept 3

States have the option of granting public employees the right to bargain, and they have the added option of deciding to exclude specific groups of public employees, such as teachers and administrators, from the right to collectively bargain. By the mid-1980's, 86 percent of the nation's public school teachers did collectively bargain with almost two million teachers belonging to either the National Education Association or the American Federation of Teachers, the two major teachers unions.

Concept 4

States that have legislated collective bargaining rights for their public employees have based their laws on the NLRA, requiring bargaining for wages, hours, and other terms and conditions of employment for private sector employees and mirroring procedures prescribed by the NLRA for the private sector.

Concept 5

States that prohibit collective bargaining for teachers cite three significant differences between the private and public sectors that support legislation prohibiting public sector collective bargaining:

a. The public sector is politically and economically different from the private sector.

b. There is a direct public interest in public sector collective bargaining.

c. The means for funding public and private sector agreements differ notably.

Concept 6

If states neither require nor forbid bargaining for teachers, school boards are at liberty to bargain collectively or individually with employees, and there are no legislated procedures and timelines to guide the process. On the other hand, if states have collective bargaining laws for public employees, including teachers, in place, school boards and teachers unions are required to comply with the laws' procedures.

Concept 7

States with public sector collective bargaining laws have usually authorized the development of labor relations boards to oversee and monitor the implementation of these laws. State employment relations boards assist and monitor the implementation of the state's collective bargaining law by:

a. determining bargaining units,

b. conducting recognition elections,

c. investigating unfair labor practices,

d. monitoring collective bargaining progress, and

e. assigning mediators, fact finders, and arbitrators as needed.

Concept 8

Workers in a given collective bargaining unit should hold positions comparable in wages, hours, and other working conditions, and should share an overall community of interests.

Concept 9

Recognition elections give prospective bargaining unit members the opportunity to choose between rival organizations, or to choose no union at all to represent them. Should a majority select a given union to represent them in collective bargaining, the employer will be bound under state law to bargain all matters regarding wages, hours, and terms and conditions of employment with the chosen representative.

Concept 10

While school administrators and human relations managers are prohibited from negotiating wages, hours, and terms and conditions of employment with individuals or groups not recognized as the official bargaining agent, neither they nor the designated union have the right or authority to silence individual or collective opinion on matters of public concern that may impinge on bargaining.

Concept 11

An agency shop clause in a contract requires every employee to pay the union an amount equal to the union's customary initiation fee and monthly dues, but it does not require any employee to become a formal member of the union, to take any oath of obligation, or to observe the internal rules and regulations of the union. However, an employee who does not officially join a union cannot be forced to contribute support for an ideological cause the employee opposes.

Concept 12

All members of a given bargaining unit, whether they join the union or not, have the right to be represented by the union in collective bargaining and all matters pertaining to contract administration. Bargaining unit members who pay no fair share fee because the contract does not have an agency shop clause are entitled to the same level of union representation as union members paying for full participation in union activities.

Concept 13

The NLRA, a model for state public sector bargaining laws, provides that an individual employee or group of employees shall have the right at any time to present grievances to their employer and to have such grievances adjusted, without the intervention of the bargaining representative, as long as the adjustment is not inconsistent with the terms of a collective bargaining contract or agreement then in effect, and if the bargaining representative has been given the opportunity to be present.

Concept 14

Employees who join the union will also have the right to fully participate in the union's decision-making processes. They will vote on the adoption or rejection of union initiatives, contract proposals, and the decision to strike. Nonmembers, even those compelled to pay fair share fees, will not have a direct say in the way the union conducts its business.

Concept 15

Management can reprimand or discipline employees who do not fulfill their contractual responsibilities. On the other hand, employees may grieve management actions that appear to violate the contract.

Concept 16

Employees have essentially two categories of rights: those created by the contract, and those created by local, state, and federal law. State and local laws and contracts can give *more* rights than those accorded by federal legislation, but they cannot give *fewer* rights, or take away rights promised under federal laws.

Concept 17

Where no collective bargaining agreement exists, or where an agreement makes no mention of a matter, the employer and employees are subject to all applicable state laws and local ordinances pertinent to wages, hours, and terms and conditions of employment. Where a collective bargaining contract exists or develops, the contract may prevail, depending on the state, over existing provisions of law except laws pertaining to (1) civil rights, (2) affirmative action, (3) unemployment compensation, (4) workers' compensation, (5) retirement of public employees, (6) residency requirements, (7) minimum education requirements, and (8) minimum standards promulgated by a state board of education.

Concept 18

If a state has a law giving public employees the right to collectively bargain, public employers such as school districts are obligated to meet in good faith with the union in order to discuss and bargain wages, hours, and terms and conditions of employment. However, unless the public employer agrees otherwise in a collective bargaining agreement, it cannot be required to bargain on any matter that impairs the right and responsibility of the employer to determine matters of inherent managerial policy.

Concept 19

In some state laws, while the decisions left to managerial discretion are not themselves bargainable, the *effect* of these decisions on the terms and conditions of employment is bargainable. For example, a school district has the right to decide to close a school, but the effect of that decision on displaced employees will be a bargainable issue.

Concept 20

Management Rights Clauses, found in many contracts, make it clear that boards of education will retain all management rights accorded them by law unless expressly limited by a provision of the negotiated contracts which the boards have signed.

Concept 21

Basically, items for negotiation can be mandatory, permissive, or forbidden. Mandatory items, such as wages, hours, and terms and conditions of employment, *must be negotiated*, and can be bargained to impasse, that is, failure to reach agreement on mandatory items can lead to a strike if the state's law permits public employees to strike. Permissive items *can be negotiated* if both parties agree to bring them to the table, but neither side has a legal duty to do so, and failure to reach agreement on permissive items cannot be a reason to strike. Permissive items brought to the table and negotiated into the contract become mandatory subjects of bargaining in future negotiations. Prohibited items are those beyond a board's power to negotiate including nondelegable management rights and civil rights protected by state and federal statutes.

Concept 22

Collectively bargained agreements, where they exist, have the force of law in prescribing and limiting both employee and management rights and responsibilities.

SUGGESTIONS FOR CLASSROOM DISCUSSION, RESEARCH, AND ACTIVITIES

1. Have students compare the form and content of a public sector collective bargaining agreement with the form and content of a comparable private sector collective bargaining agreement.

2. Have students examine state statutes dealing with public sector collective bargaining. Are teachers included in the law? If not, why not? The legislative history of these laws may provide an answer.

3. Have students research and compare the salary scales of teachers in states that allow collective bargaining with the salary scales of teachers in comparable school districts in states that prohibit collective bargaining for teachers.

4. Have students survey and compare the bargaining unit structures of at least ten different school districts. Which employees collectively bargain, and which categories of employees are members of the same bargaining units in each of the sample districts? Do they share a community of interests as prescribed by the NLRA or state law?

5. Have students survey districts that collectively bargain to determine the frequency with which *agency shop* clauses are part of the negotiated agreements.

CHAPTER 2: TEST QUESTIONS AND ANSWERS

1. Historically, the right to collectively bargain is a rather recent phenomenon. When and how did employees in the private sector win the right to bargain, and when and how did employees in the public sector first get the right to collectively bargain?

Answer: The private sector labor movement began in the middle of the nineteenth century, but it wasn't until the passage of the NLRA, also known as the Wagner Act, in 1935, that private sector employees won the right to join unions and collectively bargain. Public sector collective bargaining rights came even later. President Kennedy's Executive Order 10988 in 1962 opened the door in granting federal employees the right to join labor unions and bargain collectively. In 1968, President Nixon's Executive Order 11491 superseded Kennedy's efforts and established actual bargaining procedures and protocols that mirrored those found in the private sector.

2. Why do some states refuse to allow teachers to collectively bargain?

Answer: States prohibiting collective bargaining for teachers believe that allowing collective bargaining amounts to an illegal delegation of discretionary governing power to the teachers' union. The union, a private interest group, becomes a participant in the school board's legislative process, a public activity, in that the end effect of collective bargaining requires the public served to fund the contract developed through taxation, essentially giving the union an element of control over the fiscal resources of a community.

3. Collective bargaining laws usually share similar components. Identify the topics addressed in most collective bargaining laws.

Answer: Most collective bargaining laws discuss:

a. management rights and responsibilities;

b. employee rights and responsibilities;

c. bargaining unit definition;

d. scope of bargaining;

e. the bargaining process and timelines;

f. impasse procedures;

g. unfair labor practices;

h. grievance procedures; and

i. agency oversight, penalties, and enforcement procedures.

4. What factors are weighed in determining which workers can become members of a designated bargaining unit?

Answer: Workers in a given collective bargaining unit should hold positions comparable in wages, hours, and other working conditions, and should share an overall community of interests. In determining community of interests in the private sector, the National Labor Relations Board considers such facts as differences in employee benefits, separate supervision, degree of dissimilar qualifications, training, skills, differences in job functions, time away from employment, frequency of contact with other employees, integration of work functions, and collective bargaining history.

5. What is direct dealing, and why is it an unfair labor practice?

Answer: Discussing employment matters with individuals is considered "direct dealing," a violation of exclusivity and a recognized unfair labor practice. Individuals seeking to override group contracts will inevitably defeat the purpose of collective bargaining. They will create separate agreements ignoring collective needs and destroying labor peace.

6. How does the concept of exclusivity affect the ability of rival unions to advance their pursuit of recognition?

Answer: The concept of exclusivity can limit their channels of communication regarding labor issues. Although the recognized union may have access to the school's mailboxes, as long as other channels of communication are available, school districts are not constitutionally obligated to grant rival unions access to school mailboxes because a school's internal mail system is not a public forum. A school can, however, create a public forum by allowing the general public and all employee organizations to use its mailboxes.

7. What is the difference between the concepts of *closed shop, union shop,* and *agency shop*?

Answer: It is against the law to require employers to hire only union members. This practice, referred to as a *closed shop* is forbidden in the private sector by both the NLRA and the Taft-Hartley Amendments. In the private sector some private employers do sometimes agree to maintain *union shops,* that is, to require employees to join the designated union *after* they are employed. *Agency shop* and fair share agreements are union security provisions found in public sector negotiations requiring all members of a given bargaining unit to fiscally support the union's efforts in their behalf, by paying a fee reflecting the employee's fair share of the expenses incurred.

8. What two opportunities exist for employees to avoid paying fair share fees required by *agency shop* clauses in collectively bargained agreements?

Answer: An employee who does not officially join a union cannot be forced to contribute support for an ideological cause the employee opposes. Employees who are not members of the union can request a rebate of the portion of their fair share fees used to advance political activities or causes having no direct bearing on collective bargaining or contract administration. Employees may also object to fair share payments to unions on religious grounds. Any public employee who is a member of and adheres to established and traditional tenets or teachings of a bona fide religion or religious body that has historically held conscientious objections to joining or financially supporting an employee organization, and which is exempt from taxation under the provisions of the Internal Revenue Code, can claim this exemption.

9. Leslie Smith, a teacher in a school district whose collective bargaining agreement has no *agency shop* clause, has chosen not to join the union. Now she has received a scathing, and she believes, unfair evaluation by her building principal, and is faced with the potential of having her contract terminated at the end of the school year. Discuss Leslie's rights and the union's responsibilities in this scenario.

Answer: Bargaining unit members who pay no fair share fee because the contract does not have an *agency shop* clause are nevertheless entitled to the same level of union representation as union members paying for full participation in union activities. Unions cannot pick and choose which bargaining unit members they will represent. Once officially designated the bargaining unit representative, the union must represent *all* members recognized by a community of interests as part of the bargaining unit. Section 7 of the NLRA, on which public sector collective bargaining laws are patterned, guarantees an employee's right to the presence of a union representative at an investigatory interview in which the risk of discipline exists. The union representative safeguards not only the particular employee's interest, but also the interests of the entire bargaining unit by exercising vigilance to make certain that the employer does not initiate or continue a practice of imposing punishment unjustly.

10. Give examples of mandatory, permissive, and forbidden negotiation topics.

Answer: Wages and hours are examples of mandatory items, while class size and curriculum are permissive topics in negotiations. Prohibited items are those beyond a board's power to negotiate. These include nondelegable management rights and civil rights protected by state and federal statutes. For example, the U.S. Supreme Court overturned a collectively bargained agreement that violated the equal protection rights of nonminority teachers by protecting members of certain minority groups from layoffs.

Chapter Three

The Collective Bargaining Process

PIVOTAL CONCEPTS

This chapter explores the bargaining process itself. Preparation for negotiations, legal requirements for disclosure, and proposal and strategy development are discussed, as well as the logistics of bargaining and the need for confidentiality throughout the process. The chapter also compares adversarial and collaborative approaches to collective bargaining.

Concept 1

Probably no decision is as central to the success or failure of negotiations as the selection of negotiating team members. The teachers' union will usually be represented by its president, select teachers representing different grade levels and interests within the union, and either a lawyer or field representative hired by the state affiliate. Board teams could potentially include one or more board of education members, the superintendent, the school district's attorney, the human resource director, and one or more district administrators.

Concept 2

Negotiating teams must gather information from a variety of sources in order to develop proposals that respond to state and local pressures, and address district needs. Board and union preparation should begin with a thorough review of the existing contract, that is, what parts of the contract have caused problems, and what language has engendered grievances throughout the life of the expiring contract. Negotiators on both sides will inevitably point to wages, hours, and terms and conditions in comparable districts to support the proposals they make, therefore, negotiators should also review contracts in comparable districts.

Concept 3

Districts in states with collective bargaining laws patterned on the NLRA will be expected to respond to union requests for such information as financial statements, enrollment reports, sick leave usage reports, and benefit plan comparisons that can be used to formulate and support union bargaining. And, even in states that make no legal provision for collective bargaining, the Freedom of Information Act and comparable state public records acts provide for public disclosure of information contained in agency files, written reports, records, and budget accounts that unions will find helpful in preparing for the possibility of bargaining.

Concept 4

An essential part of preparation for negotiations is prioritizing the items on the bargaining agenda. Which items are most important to each side, and what modifications or sacrifices is each side prepared to make in order to win on high priority issues? Each side must determine what is ideal, what is acceptable, and what is unacceptable contract language addressing each issue.

Concept 5

There are basically two approaches to public school collective bargaining: the traditional or adversarial approach, and collaborative bargaining. These approaches differ in both process and goal. In adversarial bargaining the goal is partisan satisfaction, a win for one side or the other. In collaborative bargaining, the goal is mutual satisfaction.

Concept 6

In order to bargain effectively, ground rules and procedures should be developed before the process begins. Time, place, and manner of bargaining, the number of bargainers on each side, the length of bargaining sessions, and procedures for calling time for separate group discussion, or caucusing are some of the logistics of bargaining that should be agreed upon before the process begins.

Concept 7

The negotiating parties should establish a mutually agreed upon protocol for communicating with constituents and the press before negotiations begin, as part of the ground rules.

Concept 8

It is the union's goal to include all aspects of human resource management in the contract, thus legally creating a total waiver of legislated management rights. It is the board's goal to incorporate as few aspects of human resource management as possible in the contract, thereby preserving the board's legislated right to determine district employment policy.

SUGGESTIONS FOR CLASSROOM DISCUSSION, RESEARCH, AND ACTIVITIES

1. Have students decide which factors they would use in order to determine the districts that are comparable to their own for purposes of supporting bargaining positions.

2. Using these factors to guide their research, have students secure contracts from districts comparable to their own and compare clauses dealing with school calendar, teaching day, class size, assignment and transfer, leave, benefits, and salary.

3. Have students interview members of the board's bargaining team regarding preparation, perception of effectiveness, approach to bargaining, and satisfaction with the results of the last negotiating process.

4. Have students interview members of the union's bargaining team regarding preparation, perception of effectiveness, approach to bargaining, and satisfaction with results of the last negotiating process.

5. Discuss and compare information gleaned from the interviews in activities 4 and 5.

CHAPTER 3: TEST QUESTIONS AND ANSWERS

1. Discuss the pros and cons of union consultants and school district attorneys participating in negotiations.

Answer: On the positive side of the ledger, the attorneys and consultants bring obvious legal expertise and experience to the bargaining table and a show of external power. The contract will be a legal and binding document, and attorneys and consultants can play a vital role in ensuring that contract language is unambiguous and enforceable. However, a school district and union must pay for the attorney and consultant participation in negotiations, and the cost of representation at the bargaining table should be a consideration. Districts and unions should also recognize that there could be a conflict of interest for attorneys and consultants in that unclear contract language and oversights at the bargaining table will inevitably lead to more billable hours for both after ratification. One final and very important concern is that attorneys and consultants are disinterested third-party professionals, hired guns, who can leave when their job is done. They do not have to live with the contracts they help develop.

2. Compare traditional adversarial bargaining with collaborative bargaining.

Answer: In adversarial bargaining the goal is partisan satisfaction, a win for one side or the other. In interest-based collaborative bargaining, the goal is mutual satisfaction. Collective bargaining adversaries plan for bargaining by defining partisan interests, while collaborative bargainers define mutual interests and concerns. In adversarial bargaining, there is a series of give-and-take exchanges with each side yielding on some demands in return for concessions from the other side. Collaborative bargaining begins with the identification of mutual concerns, or mutual ground in resolving partisan interests. Adversaries bluff, bargain, and eventually win a partisan victory or resolve themselves to acceptable compromise. Collaborative bargainers brainstorm solutions that will bring both sides victory.

3. Develop a board of education clause regarding class size to be used in adversarial bargaining.

Answer: The board of education will attempt to limit class size to twenty-five students whenever possible.

4. Develop a union clause regarding class size to be used in adversarial bargaining.

Answer: No class shall enroll more than twenty-five students at any time, for any reason. When enrollment exceeds twenty-five students, a new class will be created.

5. Using a collaborative approach to bargaining this class size issue, brainstorm possible ways in which this issue may be resolved to the satisfaction of both sides.

Answer:

a. When class size is more than twenty-five, the teacher's pay will be supplemented to incrementally reflect added enrollment.

b. When class size is more than twenty-five, an instructional aide will be assigned to assist the teacher.

c. When class size is more than twenty-five, excess students will be assigned to classes with less than twenty-five.

(These are just three possible brainstorming options. Students may have others, and will be free to choose which option they perceive as most likely to benefit both sides.)

6. What are some of the ways in which negotiators should prepare for collective bargaining?

Answer: Board and union preparation should begin with a thorough review of the existing contract. Special attention should be given to grievances that repeatedly arise from specific contract clauses. Grievance review can red flag contract language that is perceived as ambiguous, and cleaning up such clauses should be a focus of impending negotiations. Administrators can help the board's team with this phase of preparatory research and should be polled concerning perceived problems, as well as program changes, new legal mandates, and personnel concerns unique to their buildings. Union building representatives can provide similar input for the union's team. In addition, negotiators on both sides should have a clear understanding of where the school district stands financially before negotiations begin. The district's chief financial officer, usually the treasurer, should provide this information before negotiations begin. Also, negotiators on both sides should review comparable district contracts to support the proposals they make or their decisions to reject proposals made by the other side.

7. What kinds of information must a school board provide to a union preparing to collectively bargain?

Answer: Under § 8(a)(5) of the NLRA, the prototype for most public sector collective bargaining laws, employers have a duty to provide a union with relevant information needed for the proper performance of its duties as the bargaining representative. Thus, districts in states with collective bargaining laws patterned on the NLRA will be expected to respond to union requests for such information as financial statements, enrollment reports, sick leave usage reports, and benefit plan comparisons that can be used to formulate and support union bargaining. And, even in states that make no legal provision for collective bargaining, the Freedom of Information Act and comparable state public records acts provide for public disclosure of information contained in agency files, written reports, records, and budget accounts that unions will find helpful in preparing for the possibility of bargaining.

8. How can a union compel a school district to honor its request for information pertinent to bargaining?

Answer: Boards that deny the union access to information needed to bargain will be guilty of an unfair labor practice in states with collective bargaining statutes, and a violation of the Freedom of Information Acts in states that neither provide for nor prohibit bargaining. Unions faced with resistance can file complaints with state employment relations boards or with state or federal courts.

9. What are some of the logistical considerations that should be resolved before bargaining begins?

Answer: Logistical considerations include time, frequency, length, and place of meetings, as well as other procedures noted in figure 3.7 of the text.

10. What are some alternatives for dealing with the question of confidentiality during negotiations?

Answer: Some alternatives for dealing with this sensitive issue are:

a. Neither side shall issue progress reports on negotiations until the negotiations process is completed.

b. Neither side shall issue progress reports on negotiations without the prior review and consent of the other party.

c. Parties shall issue joint reports clarifying positions taken during negotiations.

d. All press releases must be approved by both parties.

Chapter Four

Collective Bargaining and Controversy

PIVOTAL CONCEPTS

This chapter discusses the concept of good faith bargaining and the procedures used when parties find that they are no longer bargaining effectively. Mediation, fact-finding, arbitration, and strike are discussed as alternative means of resolving collective bargaining disputes. In addition, the role of grievances, unfair labor practices, and "zipper" clauses in ongoing contract administration is explored.

Concept 1

Good faith bargaining consists simply of an honest intention to engage in the bargaining process with an open mind and a sincere desire to reach agreement. The law does not mandate that the parties ultimately reach agreement, nor does it dictate the substance of the terms on which the parties must bargain.

Concept 2

Unless the public employer agrees otherwise, it cannot be required to bargain on any matter that impairs the right and responsibility of the employer to determine matters of inherent managerial policy. However, there are relatively few management or policy issues that will not in one way or another deal with wages, hours, or terms and conditions of employment. Boards that refuse to bargain with the teachers' unions on issues they perceive as management prerogatives can therefore expect to be accused of not bargaining in good faith.

Concept 3

Impasse occurs when parties are no longer willing to communicate on unresolved issues. Agreement has not been reached, yet neither party is willing to compromise. Alternative dispute resolution procedures are available to help parties at impasse reach agreement, and may include mediation, fact-finding, and arbitration in various forms and combinations.

Concept 4

It is always preferable for the parties engaged in negotiations to reach their own agreement, as opposed to having an outsider impose agreement upon them. Mediation is the form of alternative dispute resolution best designed to achieve this end. The mediator's role is that of helping the parties themselves to resolve their differences and find solutions each side can accept.

Concept 5

If mediation fails to help the parties resolve their differences, fact-finding may be required by law or contract. The fact finder's mission, however, is to gather all relevant information pertinent to the issues in conflict, and to actually propose a solution to the impasse based on this data. Fact-finding differs from mediation in two significant ways. First, the impasse resolution may be developed solely by the fact finder, and, second, the fact finder may be at liberty to release the suggested settlement to the public as well as to the parties.

Concept 6

Arbitrators are not at liberty to improvise and fashion their own solutions to the problems presented by the parties. Arbitrators choose between the solutions developed and proposed by the parties themselves. Arbitration of contract issues still in dispute takes place only at impasse, after mediation and/or fact-finding have been unsuccessfully tried. Arbitration can be advisory or binding.

Concept 7

If mediation, fact-finding, and advisory arbitration fail, and binding arbitration is not an option, teachers may strike in states that statutorily permit them to do so. A strike is a willful and concerted work stoppage. No employee, public or private, has a constitutional right to strike in concert. That right must be given by state or federal law.

Concept 8

Once the parties have ratified their settlement agreement by a vote of their respective memberships, it becomes the rule book for human resource management. While the union and the administration are required by states' collective bargaining laws to negotiate wages, hours, and terms and conditions of employment, in order to avoid midterm bargaining, some contracts contain "zipper clauses" essentially ensuring that any matter not addressed in the contract remains a management right.

Concept 9

An unfair labor practice is an act or a course of conduct by either the union or the administration that violates the existing rights accorded either party under the state's collective bargaining law. Unfair labor practice charges are filed with the state employment relations boards by either the employer or the employee union against the other party.

Concept 10

While unfair labor practices are based on violations of the collective bargaining law, grievances are based on violations of the collective bargaining agreement. Grievances must connect to specific contract clauses. An essential element of every collective bargaining agreement is the clause outlining the procedure for resolving grievances.

SUGGESTIONS FOR CLASSROOM DISCUSSION, RESEARCH, AND ACTIVITIES

1. Have students review and compare the grievance procedures outlined in several collective bargaining agreements.

2. Have students interview a teacher or school district employee who has filed a grievance concerning the process and the results.

3. Have students interview an administrator named in the grievance procedure concerning the administrator's perception of the process.

4. If possible, have students review the actual written paperwork recording the resolution of a grievance in a school district that collectively bargains.

5. Have students interview employees in a school or district that does not collectively bargain

concerning procedures used by the administration to address employee concerns.

CHAPTER 4: TEST QUESTIONS AND ANSWERS

1. How have the courts defined good faith bargaining?

Answer: The courts look to the overall conduct of a party to determine if it has actively engaged in the bargaining process with an open mind and a sincere desire to reach an agreement. The law does not mandate that the parties ultimately reach agreement, nor does it dictate the substance of the terms on which the parties must bargain. In essence, the requirements of good faith bargaining are simply that the parties manifest such an attitude and conduct that will be conducive to reaching an agreement.

2. What is impasse, and how may it be resolved?

Answer: Impasse occurs when parties are no longer willing to communicate on unresolved issues. Agreement has not been reached, yet neither party is willing to compromise. Impasse may be resolved by alternative dispute resolution procedures including mediation, fact-finding, and arbitration.

3. Distinguish between the form and function of mediation, fact-finding, and arbitration.

Answer: The mediator's role is that of helping the parties themselves resolve their differences and find solutions each side can accept. The fact finder's mission, however, is to gather all relevant information pertinent to the issues in conflict, and to actually propose a solution to the impasse based on this data. Arbitrators are not at liberty to improvise and fashion their own solutions to the problems presented by the parties. Arbitrators choose between the solutions developed and proposed by the parties themselves.

4. Arbitration may be advisory or binding. What does this mean?

Answer: Parties using advisory arbitration are under no obligation to accept the decision of the arbitrator. On the other hand, if arbitration is binding, the parties will be forced to accept the decision of the arbitrator as their final settlement and honor it for the life of the contract.

5. Why do some critics oppose the use of arbitration to settle collective bargaining impasses?

Answer: It has been suggested that the availability of binding arbitration undermines the collective bargaining process because it encourages parties to hold out, relying on the arbitrator as a substitute for meaningful negotiation. Critics maintain that binding arbitration amounts to an inappropriate delegation of power to the arbitrator who has the ultimate authority to determine important employment matters that could profoundly affect the services being provided for the public and the manner in which finite governmental revenues are to be expended.

6. How is it determined which method of alternative dispute resolution will be used to resolve collective bargaining impasses?

Answer: Some state collective bargaining laws actually prescribe alternative dispute resolution procedures. In states without such statutory prescriptions, parties are free to decide for themselves how they will resolve impasses. Often impasse resolution procedures are part of the contract about to expire.

7. Do all employees, private or public, have a right to strike?

Answer: No employee, public or private, has a constitutional right to strike in concert. That right must be given by state or federal law. Section 7 of the NLRA gave private sector employees the right to engage in concerted activities for the purpose of collective bargaining, and striking is viewed as a form of such concerted activity. State public sector collective bargaining laws may, in a similar fashion, give some or all public sector employees the right to strike, but state public sector collective bargaining laws may also specifically forbid public employee strikes.

8. What must teachers in states that allow them to strike as part of the collective bargaining process do before they legally declare a strike?

Answer: In states that do allow teachers to strike, they must usually follow certain legislated procedures. Only after the contract has expired, and the union has engaged in good faith bargaining, including the use of prescribed alternative dispute resolution procedures, does strike become an option. Even then, teachers are required to notify both the board of education and the state employee relations board of their planned work stoppage, and to provide assurances that the strike will not endanger public health or safety.

9. What is a "zipper clause," and how does it affect contract administration?

Answer: Contracts containing "zipper clauses" essentially ensure that any matter not addressed in the contract remains a management right. "Zipper clauses" give the board of education the right to act unilaterally during the life of the contract on matters that are not part of the negotiated agreement.

10. What is the difference between an unfair labor practice and a grievance?

Answer: A grievance is the mechanism for addressing a perceived breach of the contract. An unfair labor practice is an act or a course of conduct by either the union or the administration that violates the existing rights accorded either party under the state's collective bargaining law.

Chapter Five

Laws Affecting Human Resource Management

PIVOTAL CONCEPTS

This chapter explores the impact of federal and state legislation on human resource management. Although many state laws dealing with workplace issues will directly parallel federal legislation, state laws cannot accord fewer rights and privileges, and state laws can never override federal legislation. The laws selected for review in this chapter are those most likely to have an effect on human resource management in the public school setting.

Concept 1

Employees who collectively bargain are protected by the contract and by federal and state laws prescribing specific rights in the workplace. Employees who do not collectively bargain, for example, administrators and teachers in some states, rely solely on federal and state laws to prescribe and protect their rights in the workplace. The protections such federal and state laws provide cannot be overridden or ignored by local contracts, or management rights.

Concept 2

State laws can give employees more rights than those granted by federal law, but they cannot give employees fewer rights than those accorded by the Constitution and federal statutes. Title VII, Title IX, and the Americans with Disabilities Act (ADA) are examples of federal laws affecting human resource management.

Concept 3

Title VII of the Civil Rights Act of 1964 prohibits hiring, firing, promotion, demotion, and similar employment decisions based on race, color, religion, sex, or national origin.

Concept 4

Employees who believe they have been the victims of workplace discrimination can register a charge of discrimination with the Equal Employment Opportunity Commission (EEOC), the federal agency responsible for ensuring compliance with Title VII, and if it finds reasonable cause to believe that the charge has validity, the agency will try to eliminate the discriminatory practice initially by informal conferencing, conciliating, and persuading.

Concept 5

If efforts at conciliation prove unsuccessful, the EEOC may bring a civil action against the employer, or where it has reason to believe there has been a Title VII violation, the EEOC may issue the complaining employee a "right to sue letter" essentially authorizing the complaining employee to go to court and request a jury trial.

Concept 6

In order to prove a charge of employment discrimination, plaintiff employees must show that they are members of one of the classes protected by Title VII, that they applied for and were qualified for a position, that they were denied the position, and that the employer continued to seek applicants with the plaintiff's qualifications.

Concept 7

Potential remedies available under Title VII include orders to hire or reinstate with back pay. In addition, as a result of the Civil Rights Act of 1991, victims of employment discrimination may also be awarded compensatory and punitive damages if they prove that the discrimination was intentional.

Concept 8

Employees charging discrimination on the basis of race, color, creed, gender, or national origin have the burden of proving their claim. A defending employer must merely produce a nondiscriminatory reason for the employment decision in dispute, but the employer is not obligated to prove that the reason offered is legitimate and nondiscriminatory.

Concept 9

The burden is on the complaining employee to show that the reason the employer has given is false, and that the reason for the lie is intentional discrimination. Furthermore, even if the employee succeeds in proving that discrimination played a role in the disputed employment decision, an employer can still avoid liability by showing that it had other valid reasons for the decision even if discrimination did play a role in the decision-making process.

Concept 10

Affirmative action is the policy of hiring, promoting, and enhancing the employment opportunities of protected classes such as women and minorities. Affirmative action programs are detailed, result-oriented programs, which, when carried out in good faith, result in compliance with the equal opportunity clauses found in most legislative and executive orders.

Concept 11

Title VII protects the very general categories of race, religion, gender, and national origin. No specific races, religions, genders, or national origins are cited, and in recent years, there have been a number of significant reverse discrimination suits brought by Caucasians and men.

Concept 12

Title IX of the Education Amendments of 1972 prohibits gender discrimination in education programs and activities that receive federal financial assistance. In 1992, the Supreme Court used Title IX to make compensatory and punitive damages available for victims of sexual harassment.

Concept 13

There are essentially two kinds of sexual harassment. The first is referred to as *quid pro quo*, and occurs when submission or rejection of unwelcome sexual conduct is used as the basis for employment decisions. The second type of harassment subjects the victim employee to a *hostile environment* created when an employee is subjected to unwelcome sexual conduct, and the harassment is sufficiently severe or pervasive as to alter the terms or conditions of employment and create an abusive working environment.

Concept 14

Employers can avoid liability for hostile environment claims by showing that:

a. the employer exercised reasonable care to prevent and promptly correct any sexually harassing behavior, and

b. the plaintiff employee unreasonably failed to take advantage of any preventive or corrective opportunities provided by the employer or to otherwise avoid harm.

Concept 15

The Supreme Court has extended Title VII and Title IX protections against gender discrimination to cover same-sex harassment. In addition, the courts have found that a hostile environment can be created by harassing colleagues as well as supervisors.

Concept 16

The Pregnancy Act of 1978 provides that women affected by pregnancy, childbirth, or related medical conditions shall be treated the same for all employment-related purposes, including the receipt of benefits under fringe benefit programs, as other persons not so affected but similar in their ability or inability to work.

Concept 17

The Equal Pay Act makes it unlawful to pay employees of one sex more than employees of another sex where the jobs performed require equal skill, effort, and responsibility, and are performed at the same site under the same or similar working conditions.

Concept 18

Section 504 of the Rehabilitation Act of 1973 prohibits recipients of federal funding from discriminating against qualified disabled individuals with respect to recruitment, hiring, compensation, job assignment, and fringe benefits, and requires employers to provide reasonable work environment accommodations for qualified disabled applicants or employees unless these accommodations result in undue hardship for the employer.

Concept 19

The ADA extends, clarifies, and enhances the protections of Section 504. It differs from Section 504 in that it applies to both public and private sector employees, and includes provisions regarding public accommodations, public transportation, telecommunications, and the receipt of government services for the disabled.

Concept 20

The ADA prohibits discrimination against any qualified disabled individual because of the individual's disability in regard to job application procedures, hiring, advancement, discharge, compensation, job training, and other terms, conditions, and privileges of employment. Employers are expected to provide the accommodations a disabled employee will need to enter or remain in the workforce, unless the employer can show that accommodating the employee results in undue hardship.

Concept 21

The Age Discrimination in Employment Act (ADEA) prohibits any employment practices that adversely affect the job status of employees over forty, and prohibits retaliation against employees supporting the age discrimination complaints of others.

Concept 23

The Family and Medical Leave Act (FMLA) of 1993 provides nondiscriminatory leave to *men* and women to care for a newborn or adopted child, a sick spouse or parent, or the employee's own health needs. This law allows all eligible employees up to twelve work weeks per year of unpaid leave:

1. to care for a newborn child;

2. to care for, or spend additional time with, an adopted child or foster child;

3. to care for a spouse, child, or parent with a serious health condition; or

4. to recover from a serious health condition.

Concept 24

FMLA leave differs from other unpaid leave in that it comes with certain protections intended to minimize employee stress in dealing with family crisis and the demands of work. Employees returning from FMLA leave must be restored to positions previously held or to equivalent positions with the same pay, benefits, and working conditions, and with seniority and benefits accrued before the leave intact.

Concept 25

Workers' Compensation laws make the employer strictly liable to an employee for injuries sustained by the employee, which arise out of and in the course of employment, without regard to the negligence of the employer or that of the employee. Workers' compensation is an *exclusive* remedy for on-the-job injuries, and insured employers are assured that they will not have to respond to a suit and submit to the vagaries of courtroom decisions.

Concept 26

Unemployment Compensation, a function of state law for public school employees, provides employees who are laid off *through no fault of their own* with a financial subsidy to see them through the period of *involuntary* unemployment. The proverbial fly in the ointment of administrating unemployment compensation benefits lies in the determination of when an employee is *involuntarily* unemployed. Teachers who believe they have been wrongfully discharged will sue for reinstatement and to recoup lost unemployment compensation benefits.

Concept 27

COBRA, the Consolidated Omnibus Budget Reconciliation Act of 1985, provides that unless an employee has been released for "gross misconduct," the employee is entitled to continue participation in the district's group health plan for a period up to eighteen months. The employee's spouse and dependent children are also entitled to continued coverage in such plans for up to thirty-six months, if they would otherwise lose coverage due to the death of the covered employee, divorce or legal separation, or leaving dependency status. The premiums for continued coverage, however, must be paid for by the employee, spouse, or child, unless the employer has agreed otherwise, and may be up to 102 percent of the regular group rate.

Concept 28

The Fourteenth Amendment is a protective catchall, assuring public school employees that they will be entitled to all the rights and benefits provided by the Constitution and federal laws no matter where they work, and assuring them fair treatment when they are threatened with the loss of life, liberty, or property interests, such as jobs, salaries, and benefits of employment. The Fourteenth Amendment, which accords employees both *substantive* and *procedural due process*, comes into play when teachers are disciplined, dismissed, or nonrenewed.

Concept 29

Procedural due process equates with fair treatment and requires:

1. notice of the reason for the adverse action taken;

2. an opportunity to respond to these reasons and charges;

3. the opportunity to confront and cross-examine witnesses;

4. the opportunity to be represented by counsel; and

5. the opportunity to appeal an adverse decision.

Concept 30

A *property* interest is a legitimate claim of entitlement to continued employment that is created by state law, and a teacher's property interest in a particular position comes into being when a teacher is tenured. *Liberty* interests include such fundamental constitutional rights as freedom of expression and association, but also include a teacher's freedom to take advantage of employment opportunities.

SUGGESTIONS FOR CLASSROOM DISCUSSION, RESEARCH, AND ACTIVITIES

1. Have students do a personnel inventory of teachers and classified staff assigned to their buildings, noting race, gender, and age of all employees, and discuss any perceived imbalances.

2. Have students interview their districts' human resource managers regarding the district's affirmative action plan. What specific steps are presently being taken to assure equal employment opportunities?

3. Have students review and analyze their districts' employment applications for illegal or inappropriate questions and statements.

4. Have students review and compare their districts' sexual harassment policies.

5. Have students review the salaries for coaches and stipends for supplemental positions in their districts with respect to gender and the requirements of the Equal Pay Act.

CHAPTER 5: TEST QUESTIONS AND ANSWERS

1. What does Title VII specifically prohibit, and what agency enforces this law?

Answer: The law says that a public school, or any other publicly funded institution, cannot discriminate against an individual with respect to compensation, terms, conditions, or privileges of employment because of the individual's race, color, religion, sex, or national origin. This means public schools cannot limit, segregate, or classify employees in any way that would affect an employee's job status or cause the employee to lose job opportunities. Employees who believe they have been the victims of workplace discrimination can register a charge of discrimination with the EEOC, the federal agency responsible for ensuring compliance with Title VII.

2. What must an employee do in order to win a discrimination lawsuit?

Answer: In order to prove a charge of employment discrimination, plaintiff employees must show that they are members of one of the classes protected by Title VII, that they applied for and were qualified for a position, that they were denied the position, and that the employer continued to seek applicants with the plaintiff's qualifications. This same approach, the development of a prima facie case of Title VII discrimination, will be required when employees dispute promotions, tenure, nonrenewal and discipline, termination, or other terms and conditions of employment they perceive to be discriminatory. Employees charging discrimination on the basis of race, color, creed, gender, or national origin have the burden of proving their claims. A defending employer must merely produce a nondiscriminatory reason for the employment decision in dispute, but the employer is not obligated to prove that the reason offered is legitimate and nondiscriminatory. The burden is on the complaining employee to show that the reason the employer has given is false, and that the reason for the lie is intentional discrimination. Furthermore, even if the employee succeeds in proving that discrimination played a role in the disputed employment decision, an employer can still avoid liability by showing that it had other valid reasons for the decision even if discrimination did play a role in the decision-making process.

3. What steps has the EEOC recommended employers take to establish affirmative action programs?

Answer: The EEOC has disseminated the following guidance for employers who wish to establish affirmative action programs:

a. Develop and disseminate a written policy assuring that there will be no discrimination in employment practices.

b. Appoint a director to oversee administration of this policy.

c. Analyze staffing with respect to the number of females and minorities employed.

d. In light of this analysis, develop measurable remedial goals for hiring, and a timetable for achieving these goals.

e. Develop and implement specific programs to eliminate discrimination in employment.

f. Review employment selection processes with respect to their direct and disparate impact on protected classes.

g. Conduct internal audits to monitor employment practices.

h. Develop district and community programs that support affirmative action goals.

4. What is sexual harassment as proscribed by Title IX?

Answer: Sexual harassment in the workplace is any unwelcome sexual advance, request for sexual favors, or other verbal or physical conduct of a sexual nature.

5. What is the difference between *quid pro quo* and *hostile environment* sexual harassment?

Answer: *Quid pro quo* harassment occurs when submission or rejection of unwelcome sexual conduct is used as the basis for employment decisions. With this type of harassment, the employee is injured in that they are forced to submit or become the victim of an adverse employment decision. The second type of harassment, on the other hand, may not result in an actual loss or injury, but rather subjects the victim employee to a *hostile environment.* A hostile environment is created when an employee is subjected to unwelcome sexual conduct, and the harassment is sufficiently severe or pervasive as to alter the terms or conditions of employment and create an abusive working environment.

6. How can employers avoid liability for hostile environment sexual harassment?

Answer: Employers avoid liability by showing:

a. that the employer exercised reasonable care to prevent and promptly correct any sexually harassing behavior, and

b. that the plaintiff employee unreasonably failed to take advantage of any preventive or corrective opportunities provided by the employer or to otherwise avoid harm.

7. How does the ADA address the health problems presented by alcoholism, drug addiction, and HIV infection?

Answer: The ADA protects *recovered* alcoholics and drug addicts from employment discrimination. It does not, however, protect active users. Reasonable drug testing is permitted to confirm that an individual is not using drugs, because current drug use is not protected by the ADA. The ADA does protect employees infected with the HIV virus, requiring that the infected employee receive the reasonable accommodations needed to perform the essential functions of employment, and assurances of confidentiality.

8. What are some examples of the reasonable accommodations required by the ADA?

Answer: The kinds of accommodations that are to be available include:

a. making existing facilities readily accessible to and usable by disabled persons;

b. job restructuring;

c. part-time or modified work schedules;

d. reassignment to a vacant position;

e. acquisition or modification of equipment or devices;

f. appropriate adjustment or modifications of examinations, training materials, or policies;

g. the provision of qualified readers or interpreters; and

h. other similar accommodations.

9. Describe the benefits provided by the FMLA.

Answer: This law allows all eligible employees up to twelve work weeks per year of unpaid leave:

a. to care for a newborn child;

b. to care for, or spend additional time with, an adopted child or foster child;

c. to care for a spouse, child, or parent with a serious health condition; or

d. to recover from a serious health condition.

FMLA leave can be taken all at once, or intermittently. Employees taking FMLA leave retain their health benefits throughout the leave period. More importantly, employees returning from FMLA leave must be restored to positions previously held, or to equivalent positions with the same pay, benefits, and working conditions, and with seniority and benefits accrued before the leave intact.

10. Differentiate between Workers' Compensation and Unemployment Compensation laws.

Answer: Workers' Compensation laws make employers strictly liable to employees for injuries sustained by employees, which arise out of and in the course of employment, without regard to the negligence of the employers or that of the employees. Unemployment Compensation laws provide employees who are laid off *through no fault of their own* a financial subsidy to see them through the period of *involuntary* unemployment.

Chapter Six

Planning and Recruitment

PIVOTAL CONCEPTS

Law, contract, district input, and current personnel status all must be addressed in projecting staffing for a sound educational program. This chapter discusses the role of these factors in planning for personnel needs. Job description development, *bona fide occupational qualifications* (BFOQ), job advertisements, and the general application process are also reviewed from a legal perspective.

Concept 1

The number of administrators, teachers, and support staff needed to implement an educational program will be influenced by legislation, contract, district goals and profiles, and the status of personnel already employed.

Concept 2

State laws can fully control what is taught and how it is taught, and, in so doing, have a direct effect on a school district's staffing. School districts are required to develop programs and hire teachers to address state concerns. Safety, health, and educational standards set by state law will limit the size of classes and the number of teacher assignments in a given school day.

Concept 3

In school districts that collectively bargain, negotiated contracts frequently set limits on class size, the number of instructional assignments teachers can receive, and the way in which substitute coverage will be provided. These factors, as well as sick leave, pregnancy leave, and personal leave provisions in state laws and district contracts, have a direct effect on school staffing needs and personnel planning.

Concept 4

Part of the planning function should be the development of a community profile, which includes community input through school district surveys and community studies. School districts must assess present and potential community growth as a pivotal part of their own personnel planning function.

Concept 5

An integral part of planning for staffing involves assessing the status of those already employed in a district. Projected use of sick leave, pregnancy leave, and retirement will all affect staffing.

Concept 6

The process of recruitment must include the development of job descriptions, official and legally binding statements describing a position's qualifications and responsibilities. Job descriptions require the employing district to clarify its expectations, and they require the applicant to attest to qualifications and abilities that address those stated expectations. Job descriptions should include school mission statements and objectives, qualifications, responsibilities, outcomes, and evaluation criteria.

Concept 7

Discrimination can sometimes be found in job descriptions that include physical or performance demands that tend to preclude members of protected classes from applying. Disparate impact claims are usually based on statistics showing that, despite the intent of the employer, members of a protected class were the victims of discrimination as the result of the employer's business practices. Employers are allowed to maintain otherwise discriminatory employment practices only if they can show that such practices and policies are job-related and consistent with business necessity, and that there is no alternative employment practice available that would be equally effective and have a less discriminatory impact.

Concept 8

The ADA, the ADEA, and the Pregnancy Act protect the disabled, those over forty, and pregnant women from employment decisions that may have a disparate impact on their employment opportunities. It is rare in public education for race, creed, gender, national origin, age, or pregnancy to rise to the level of a BFOQ.

Concept 9

Stated qualifications and responsibilities must be related to the job in order to be considered a BFOQ. The job description should state all degrees, certifications, skills and training needed for a given position, and position responsibilities and objectives, and the position should be filled by whichever applicant best fits the published job description.

Concept 10

An organizational chart illustrates a district's responsibility and reporting structure. Salaries will usually be linked to job descriptions and qualifications. Positions requiring more rigorous qualifications and more extensive experience usually come with greater degrees of responsibility, and therefore merit higher pay. In public schools, salary scales correlate monetary compensation for teachers with education and experience.

Concept 11

The same laws that legislate against discriminatory concerns in the development of the job description, apply to the development of the job advertisement. School districts must be mindful of advertisements that may have a disparate impact on applicants in protected categories. In districts with a history of discriminatory hiring, an affirmative action plan may require that districts advertise in minority newspapers and use minority placement centers in order to actively pursue compliance with EEOC affirmative action guidelines.

Concept 12

A rule of thumb in constructing a district's job application is that no questions irrelevant to the position should ever be asked. Resumes and applications serve as a check on each other, and a resume provides insight into what the applicant perceives to be important, as well as the applicant's personal penchant for organization and presentation.

Concept 13

Official transcripts are an essential part of the application process. They are an official record of the applicant's academic performance, and an indicator of persistence and dedication to a task.

Concept 14

Citizenship and certification can be requirements for a teaching position. Certification or licensing indicates the completion of a college degree that includes a stated number of credits or courses in education, including applicable field experiences, and proof of good character.

Concept 15

Teaching certificates have been found by the courts to be licenses, subject to state renewal requirements. Teachers who do not renew their teaching licenses prior to expiration can be fired, and should not be hired.

SUGGESTIONS FOR CLASSROOM DISCUSSION, RESEARCH, AND ACTIVITIES

1. Have students review and compare advertisements for teaching positions with respect to qualifications and job requirements.

2. Have students review and compare advertisements for administrative positions with respect to qualifications, job requirements, and salaries.

3. Have students compare administrative salaries to teacher salaries in their districts.

4. Have students prepare personal resumes.

5. Have students review and compare resumes for style and content.

CHAPTER 6: TEST QUESTIONS AND ANSWERS

1. What are some of the factors to consider in developing a community profile?

Answer: Population, Major Business and Industries, Average Family Size and Income, and other factors listed in figure 6.3 of the text.

2. What are some of the factors a human resource manager must consider in developing a legally defensible job description?

Answer: Job descriptions that are legally defensible require an analysis of the following job features:

a. What are the responsibilities of the position?

b. Why are these responsibilities significant to the position?

c. How should performance of these responsibilities be evaluated?

d. What skills are needed for this position?

e. What educational background is required for this position?

f. What job specific training and experience are required for this position?

g. How does this job relate to the work of others?

h. What physical demands will be placed on the successful applicant?

i. What environmental conditions will affect performance?

j. How will performance be evaluated?

3. What is meant by disparate impact discrimination in employment?

Answer: This kind of discrimination can sometimes be found in job descriptions that include physical or performance demands that tend to preclude members of protected classes from applying. Disparate impact claims are usually based on statistics showing that, despite the intent of the employer, members of a protected class were the victims of discrimination as the result of the employer's business practices. Employers are allowed to maintain otherwise discriminatory employment practices only if they can show that such practices and policies are job-related and consistent with business necessity, and that there is no alternative employment practice available that would be equally effective and have a less discriminatory impact. Employees win disparate impact cases by showing that the employer refused to adopt other equally effective practices that would not have a discriminatory effect, or that the employer's policy was not job-related or a business necessity.

4. Give an example of a BFOQ?

Answer: It is legitimate to require a special education teacher in a self-contained program for severely disabled students to be able to lift 200 pounds or more if the teacher will be expected to help students move from desk to wheel chair. This qualification may eliminate teachers who are themselves disabled from the applicant pool, however, the qualification in this instance is indeed a business necessity, a BFOQ.

5 Can a school district require applicants to submit to a medical exam as part of the application process?

Answer: School districts can require a medical exam *after* a contract has been offered, if all employees are subject to the same requirement.

6. Can a school district refuse to honor a contract offered to a teacher who tests positive for drug use during a medical exam required *after* the contract has been offered?

Answer: Yes. Employees who are currently using drugs are not protected by the ADA, and school districts are not required to reasonably accommodate drug users.

7. Can race ever be an issue or BFOQ in school district hiring?

Answer: In districts with a history of discriminatory hiring, an affirmative action plan may require that districts advertise in minority newspapers and use minority placement centers in order to actively pursue compliance with EEOC guidelines. Essentially, districts with a past history of discriminatory hiring may be required to hire minorities in order to make up for past practices.

8. What five elements should be included in the teacher application process?

Answer: The teacher application process should include all of the following elements:

a. a completed and signed district application form;

b. an applicant resume;

c. a copy of a valid teaching certificate;

d. an official copy of all undergraduate and graduate transcripts; and

e. a copy of National Teacher Examination scores.

9. Which of the following application questions is illegal?

a. What organizations do you belong to?

b. How did you learn to speak Spanish?

c. Are you a United States citizen?

Answer:

a. What organizations do you belong to? [Illegal]

b. How did you learn to speak Spanish? [Illegal]

c. Are you a United States citizen? [Legal]

10. What are some of the reasons for which a state may revoke a teacher's license to teach?

Answer: States have the authority to revoke teacher licenses for a variety of reasons, including immorality, incompetency, breach of contract, and neglect of duty. There is no single definitive list of reasons for revocation, but license revocation can be based on a teacher's behavior both inside and outside of the classroom.

Chapter Seven

Review, Interview, and Selection

PIVOTAL CONCEPTS

This chapter deals with the credential review and reference checking that must precede the selection of candidates for the interviewing process. The chapter also provides a roadmap for preparing the interview team for its mission, the selection of the best candidate for the advertised position. Review, interview, and selection are explored from a legal perspective.

Concept 1

There are no secrets in human resource management. It is a business built on formality, and every form reviewed in the application process becomes a public record, accessible to the general public, including rejected applicants. The fairness and equity of the selection process are always open to public review.

Concept 2

Qualifications must always be evaluated with reference to the posted job description. Once candidates who are qualified for the advertised position are identified, the next step in the process of review is to rate and rank the applicants based on their submitted paperwork.

Concept 3

The completed application serves as a starting point for reference checking, asking applicants to name former employers, places, and periods of employment, and to provide addresses and phone numbers. Gaps in an applicant's employment history should send up a red flag.

Concept 4

Human resource managers are often called upon to both give and receive references for job applicants. The law of defamation recognizes a *qualified privilege* to tell the whole truth in situations such as these. A qualified privilege exists whenever a statement is made in good faith, without actual malice, on a subject in which the speaker has a valid interest or duty, to a person having a corresponding interest or duty.

Concept 5

When school districts simply don't bother checking the backgrounds of prospective employees by not asking for references, they can and should be held liable for the tortuous acts of those unchecked employees. To establish a cause of action for negligent hiring, a plaintiff must show that the employer knew or, in the exercise of ordinary care should have known, that an employee was unfit or dangerous at the time of the employee's hiring, and that the employee was the proximate cause of the plaintiff's injuries.

Concept 6

Telephone reference checks are the local district's required effort to check the validity of information the applicant has provided. References, their relationship to the applicant, and the period of contact should be identified, and the same questions regarding performance should be asked of each person interviewed.

Concept 7

Principals, teachers, board members, parents, and students all qualify as stakeholders and legitimate members of committees that interview prospective administrators and teachers. It is important to provide preliminary training for the interview committee that will help them understand how various state and federal laws will affect pre-employment questioning.

Concept 8

In the interest of fairness and equity, each candidate should be asked the same questions, preferably in the same sequence, and by the same committee members. Standardizing the interview process is an important part of avoiding discriminatory behavior.

Concept 9

At the end of each interview, committee members will be asked to use the information they have gleaned from the interview to numerically rate the candidates. It is best if these evaluations are done without group discussion that may pollute the process and introduce discriminatory perceptions and comments.

Concept 10

Final selection of the successful candidate for any position in a public school should rest on the objective, personal, numerical rankings assigned each candidate by the members of the interviewing committee. Selection based on any other criteria is open to criticism in that it ignores concerns for fairness, equity, and independent input in the selection process.

Concept 11

Every valid contract requires offer and acceptance. Contracts also require consideration for services rendered. In public education, successful candidates should be offered contracts clearly specifying job expectations and clarifying the salary and benefits to be received. The authority to select and appoint teachers is vested solely in the board of education, and the board carries the ultimate responsibility in all matters relating to the employment and reemployment of teachers. This power may not be delegated to the superintendent of schools or to any other person.

Concept 12

The files of finalists, those interviewed but not chosen, should not be discarded. It is wise to keep these files, arranged according to their final numerical ranking for at least one year, should something go awry or additional needs arise. A record of objective recruitment evaluation and selection is the best defense to charges of discrimination, corruption, nepotism, or inconsistency.

SUGGESTIONS FOR CLASSROOM DISCUSSION, RESEARCH, AND ACTIVITIES

1. Have students develop interview questions for the position of human resource manager.

2. Have students develop a corresponding interview rating form for the position of human resource manager.

3. Have students conduct a mock interview for the position of human resource manager following the procedures outlined in this chapter.

4. Have students conduct mock reference checks on each other and discuss the responses they received.

5. Have students discuss their own best and worst interviewing experiences.

CHAPTER 7: TEST QUESTIONS AND ANSWERS

1. Why are application deadlines an important part of a fair and equitable review process?

Answer: In order to keep the process on schedule, human resource administrators must set deadlines for submission, and, in order to avoid the perception of discriminatory treatment, human resource administrators must remain faithful to those deadlines.

2. Why are there no secrets in human resource management?

Answer: Human resource management is a business built on formality, and every form reviewed in the application process becomes a public record, accessible to the general public, including rejected applicants.

3. What is the concept of Groupthink and why is it an important consideration when structuring interviews?

Answer: Groupthink occurs when decision-making groups are cohesive, insulated from outside criticism, and subject to strong directive leadership by one or more group members. Vocal members with strong opinions essentially silence less vocal members of the group by creating an illusion of group unanimity. Individual members of the group assume that everyone else is in agreement, and that the silence of others implies consent and agreement with whatever opinions are on the table, and with whatever decisions are made. Group members invent justifications for whatever actions they take, and dismiss rival or critical opinions. In the end, the need to belong overrides the need to be true to one's own beliefs. Decisions made in an environment that fosters groupthink are more likely to be poor because *the group* is keeping individuals from evaluating and sincerely choosing among alternatives. Groupthink uses the desire for social acceptance to stifle the criticism and dissent central to finding the best solution to a problem. In human resource management, groupthink can also set the stage for stereotyping, and the discussion of factors prohibited by law.

4. Discuss the definitions and importance of proper use of the terms *arrested* and *convicted,* and *crime* and *felony* as they appear on school district application forms.

Answer: Every candidate should be asked if they have been *convicted* of a crime. There is a difference between being *arrested* and being *convicted.* A person can be arrested and, through the judicial process, be found innocent of the charge filed. However, a person who has been *convicted* of a crime has been found guilty as charged in a court of law. While it would be unfair to remove an applicant who had been arrested from consideration, convicted felons should have no place in a public school's job pool. It is also important to use the term *crime,* as opposed to *felony,* in posing this question, because many felony charges, especially sex offenses, are reduced to misdemeanors as part of plea bargaining agreements.

5. Explain the concept of *qualified privilege*.

Answer: Human resource managers are often called upon to both give and receive references for job applicants. The law of defamation recognizes a *qualified privilege* to tell the whole truth in situations such as these. A qualified privilege exists whenever a statement is made in good faith, without actual malice, on a subject in which the speaker has a valid interest or duty, to a person having a corresponding interest or duty.

6. How does an injured plaintiff win a lawsuit charging a school district with negligent hiring?

Answer: To establish a cause of action for negligent hiring, a plaintiff must show that the employer knew or, in the exercise of ordinary care should have known, that an employee was unfit or dangerous at the time of the employee's hiring, and that the employee was the proximate cause of the plaintiff's injuries. School districts that do not check references can be found guilty of negligent hiring.

7. The chapter discusses resources to help school districts conduct background checks before hiring. Describe these resources.

Answer: The Teacher Identification Clearinghouse, maintained by the National Association of State Directors of Teacher Education and Certification (NASDTEC), provides a nationwide database of teachers whose certifications have been denied, revoked, or suspended over the past ten years. States, not individual districts, join the clearinghouse, which distributes a monthly update of the names, known aliases, birth dates, and Social Security numbers of all persons whose certification was withheld by member states, and as of July 1990, forty-two states had signed clearinghouse agreements. For districts who are not members of the clearinghouse, *The Guide to Background Investigations*, referenced in this chapter, outlines procedures for obtaining criminal, court, workers' compensation, education, and driving records, and gives each state's policies regarding access to this information.

8. What are the five steps required for an equitable interviewing process?

Answer:

a. selecting the interview committee;

b. training the interview committee;

c. developing the interview questions;

d. conducting the interview and numerically rating applicants; and

e. numerical tallying and selection.

9. What are some areas interview teams should focus on in developing questions for teacher applicants?

Answer: In interviewing prospective teachers, these areas might include questions about teaching methodology, curriculum, student discipline, communications with parents, and familiarity with technology, as well as the applicant's attitudes regarding multiculturalism, professional growth, and accountability. In addition, candidates can be asked to prepare unstructured responses to situational problems posed by the interview committee.

10. Why is individual numerical ranking of applicants essential to equitable selection?

Answer: Final selection of the successful candidate for any position in a public school should rest on the objective, personal, and numerical rankings assigned each candidate by the members of the interviewing committee. Selection based on any other criteria is open to criticism in that it ignores concerns for fairness, equity, and independent input in the selection process. It sets the stage for ethical and legal challenges.

Chapter Eight

Welcoming New Employees

PIVOTAL CONCEPTS

Induction is a process, not an event. This chapter discusses the legal and pragmatic role the employee induction process plays in effective human resource management. Guides are presented for orientation and mentor program planning, and for the ongoing orientation of teaching, classified, and administrative employees.

Concept 1

Induction programs help new employees make a comfortable transition into their new assignments by acquainting them with school and community, introducing them to colleagues, providing them with necessary information and giving them the material and resource support they will need to succeed. The National Association of Secondary School Principals actually considers induction a continuation of teacher education with a significant amount of learning taking place during the process.

Concept 2

Induction is not an event. Induction is a process that translates system philosophy into cultural reality by describing and interpreting roles, relationships, and behaviors necessary for individual, unit, and organizational effectiveness. Educational administrators are always in search of the silver bullet, the single event that will do everything for everyone, but educational problems are rarely resolved by a single meeting, no matter how long or presumably informative.

Concept 3

Often districts compress the orientation process into one- or two-day programs that rarely give new employees time to breathe let alone assimilate information and adapt to their new roles and communities. Programs that are too rushed and overwhelming with information become part of the very problem induction hopes to resolve. Such programs produce confusion and frustration, as well as a first impression of district insensitivity that may last for a very long time.

Concept 4

If orientation programs are to be effective, participants must be comfortable. Heating, lighting, audiovisual preparedness, organized distributions, and food are an essential part of the orientation planning process.

Concept 5

Questions, concerns, and problems will inevitably arise in the course of ongoing employment, and so ongoing induction activities should be planned. Day-to-day induction will also occur if teachers have time and a place to meet, talk, and exchange information in an informal setting, and have resources directed at professional assimilation and growth.

Concept 6

Principals should have daily personal contact, even if only brief encounters, with every teacher in a given school.

Concept 7

Ongoing professional induction encourages new teachers to log pivotal events in that first year of service and their reaction to those events. Successful professional induction creates reflective practitioners. Every teacher, but particularly those new to the profession and the school, should be encouraged to examine what they do and the environment in which they are asked to work, i.e., to become reflective practitioners.

Concept 8

Mentoring helps beginning professionals acquire increased teaching competence, but questions of who should mentor, what training they should have, and how a mentoring program should be implemented are central to providing effective mentoring for new teachers.

Concept 9

Not every experienced teacher should be a mentor. The most important qualities for effective mentors are good communication skills, outstanding classroom skills, the respect of their peers, and the desire to participate in a mentoring program. Mentor training should include instruction in the techniques of lesson planning, clinical supervision, application of Bloom's Taxonomy, data gathering, lesson analysis, conferencing, and cognitive coaching.

Concept 10

Mentoring requires clear role definition. Mentors exist to assist, not to assess. At no time are they part of the evaluation process. Evaluation is a legally prescribed activity that is the province of licensed administrators, not teachers.

Concept 11

At the end of that critical first year, new teachers should be given the opportunity to comment on the mentoring experience, and their comments should be the basis for program adjustments.

Concept 12

Classified staff includes the school secretaries, custodians, bus drivers, cafeteria workers, and clerks. Classified employees are grouped by job description, and sometimes by bargaining unit. Just as for new teachers, orientation programs should induct new classified employees into the social and performance-related aspects of the job.

Concept 13

Administrative induction programs should prepare administrators to become macro- as opposed to micromanagers, informed and capable problem solvers. Mentoring can help new administrators adjust to their new roles.

Concept 14

Induction programs, as all school programs, should be evaluated annually. This feedback should then become part of the planning for subsequent induction programs for each group. It is also wise to involve new employees who have participated in recent induction programs directly in the planning and implementation of subsequent programs.

Concept 15

Schools have an obligation to provide employees hired after the school year has begun with some form of orientation and induction. Induction programs are the district's forum for giving new employees official notice of rules, regulations, procedures, and expectations tied to their respective new positions. The official notice new employees receive during induction becomes the legal foundation for holding them accountable for their performance.

SUGGESTIONS FOR CLASSROOM DISCUSSION, RESEARCH, AND ACTIVITIES

1. Have students design an induction program for an employee group to which they do not belong, i.e., secretaries, educational aides, or custodians.

2. Have students interview veteran members of this group in order to determine what information must be included in the program.

3. Have students discuss the legal issues that must be addressed in the induction program planned for this group.

4. Have students design an instrument for evaluating the effectiveness of the induction program they've designed.

5. Have students investigate the feasibility of videotaping this induction program for employees hired later in the school year.

CHAPTER 8: TEST QUESTIONS AND ANSWERS

1. What should be the stated objectives of an induction program for teachers?

Answer: The stated objectives of any induction program for teachers should be:

a. to improve teacher effectiveness;

b. to encourage teacher retention by giving support and assistance;

c. to promote the professional and personal well-being of new teachers;

d. to communicate district and school culture; and

e. to satisfy state mandates.

2. What are some of the basic pieces of administrative information every new teacher should receive at orientation?

Answer: Teacher assignment, negotiated agreement, teacher handbook, student handbook, curriculum, keys, texts, and other items listed in figure 8.1 of the text.

3. What are some of the *comfort* factors that must be considered in planning a successful induction program?

Answer: Each day of orientation should include some opportunity for informal human contact and physical activity as opposed to prolonged lecturing. In addition, heating, lighting, audiovisual preparedness, organized distributions, and food are an essential part of the orientation planning process.

4. How can administrators plan for the ongoing socialization central to effective induction?

Answer: Day-to-day induction will occur if teachers have time and a place to meet, talk, and exchange information in an informal setting. Teachers' lounges that are clean, comfortable, and convenient can provide that kind of setting for important ongoing socialization and induction. Community newspapers, professional journals, newsletters, computers with Internet connections, and up-to-date bulletin boards posting professional notices and opportunities should be placed in teachers' lounges to create an environment in which social and professional interests can both be nurtured. Similarly, an up-to-date teacher/school employee directory with photos and basic facts about each staff member's subject area, years in the system, and outside interests can help new staff get to know their colleagues, and school newsletters announcing births, engagements, weddings, and retirements will continue this process of socialization. Also, a social committee assigned the task of acknowledging milestones in the lives of staff with token gifts and get-togethers is a keystone in creating a culture of sustained camaraderie.

5. How can portfolio development become an induction tool for new teachers?

Answer: Portfolio development encourages new teachers to become reflective practitioners who examine, log, and write about pivotal events in their first year of service.

6. What are some of the items that should be included in a new teacher's induction year portfolio?

Answer: A portfolio plan for new teachers might include logged entries addressing the following areas:

a. a record of critical incidents and teacher responses to those incidents;

b. a list of perceived personal and professional achievements in the first year of performance;

c. a list of emerging concerns arising out of the teacher's first year of performance;

d. the teacher's objectives for addressing those concerns in the near future; and

e. a plan for evaluating objective attainment.

7. Describe the ideal mentor teacher.

Answer: The most important qualities for effective mentors are good communication skills, outstanding classroom skills, the respect of their peers, and the desire to participate in a mentoring program. Research indicates that mentors succeed when they are older than the teachers they work with, are of the same gender, and teach in the same discipline.

8. A job description for a mentoring teacher would include providing assistance in what areas?

Answer: New teachers have been found to need help in handling discipline, classroom management, lesson planning, understanding written and unwritten school rules, developing social skills, and developing techniques for handling parent conferences.

9. Define the term "classified staff" as used in this chapter.

Answer: Classified staff include any of the myriad of nonteaching, unlicensed employees who provide the support services needed to effectively run a public school. They include the school secretaries, custodians, bus drivers, cafeteria workers, and clerks. Classified employees are grouped by job description and sometimes by bargaining unit.

10. What should be the objectives for administrative induction programs?

Answer: Effective administrative induction will do five things:

a. It will introduce the new administrator to the culture of the district and the school.

b. It will define the role of the administrator in that culture.

c. It will introduce and explain administrative procedures and protocols.

d. It will highlight available resources.

e. It will give the new administrator a framework for addressing and resolving day-to-day problems.

Chapter Nine

Supervision and Evaluation

PIVOTAL CONCEPTS

This chapter deals with the supervision and evaluation functions of human resource management, differentiating between their form and focus. The chapter introduces both formal and informal models for supervising teachers and discusses the legal feasibility of using each to help teachers improve their performance. The concept of remediable and irremediable behavior is explored in light of teachers' contractual and legislated rights. In addition, the need to supervise classified and nonteaching employees, as well as teachers, is addressed, and methods for the effective supervision of these employee groups are introduced.

Concept 1

Evaluations are summative comments and opinions of a teacher's performance at the end of a given period of time, while supervision is a formative sharing of information and insights intended to improve teacher performance during that given period of time. Supervision is a process. Evaluation is an event.

Concept 2

Supervision and remediation should be guided by the district's evaluation instrument and procedures. Areas in which a teacher's performance is rated unsatisfactory on an evaluation are areas that should be the focus of supervision and remediation.

Concept 3

Tenure statutes passed in the late 1970s have been interpreted by the courts in the 1990s as requiring proof of remediation in nonrenewal and dismissal proceedings. Remediation is supervision for needed improvement, an action plan, and resources for resolving recognized problems.

Concept 4

Not every objectionable or unsatisfactory employee practice is remediable. Objectionable or unsatisfactory practices that can be eliminated or improved are considered remediable. Sexual impropriety, criminal acts, and unethical conduct are seldom remediable, while incompetence usually is remediable. Poor lesson planning or lesson execution are examples of teacher behaviors that are remediable. With proper warnings, instruction, modeling, and time, most teachers can learn to plan and execute effective lessons.

Concept 5

Irremediable behaviors are those that damage students, faculty, and schools, or that make it impossible for the offending teacher to be effective. The effects of irremediable behavior cannot be corrected. Teachers convicted of crimes are usually deemed to have engaged in irremediable behavior, although the types of crimes may differ significantly.

Concept 6

Teachers are eligible for two kinds of contracts: limited and continuing. Teachers with limited contracts are hired on an annual basis, have no property right to continued employment when the school year is over, and are said to be nontenured. Teachers with limited contracts can have their contracts nonrenewed at the end of any school year. In contrast, tenured teachers have continuing contracts, the expectation of reemployment from one year to the next, and a constitutional right to due process of law before their employment may be terminated. Tenured teachers can only be terminated for just cause, as delineated by state law and proven by a board of education.

Concept 7

Teachers attain tenure based on the status of their licenses, the quality of their teaching, and their years of successful service in a given district. Most state tenure laws prescribe a process including evaluation, and sometimes remediation, before tenure is awarded or denied. When tenure is denied, records of evaluation and remediation will come into question as school districts attempt to prove compliance with the states' teacher tenure laws.

Concept 8

Negotiated agreements or board of education policy will usually control the evaluation of teachers on continuing contract. Evaluation can be considered a term or condition of employment and therefore a bargainable issue in states that allow teachers to collectively bargain. In states where teachers do not collectively bargain, evaluation procedures will remain management's prerogative.

Concept 9

Tenured teachers have a property right to their jobs and a constitutional right to due process of law before they lose those jobs. Tenured teachers enjoy the same contractual and legal protections when faced with the threat of disciplinary action falling short of actual dismissal.

Concept 10

Nontenured teachers threatened with termination *before* their yearly contracts have expired have a right to procedural due process because such dismissal without just cause would be a breach of contract.

Concept 11

Good supervision and regular evaluation inform instructional practice. The quality of suggestions and the persuasiveness of the evaluator's rationale for improvement during supervision will determine the value of the evaluation for teachers.

Concept 12

Classroom observations entail spending the requisite period of time needed to view the presentation, implementation, and assessment of an identified instructional objective. The length of such an "official" observation may be defined by law or contract. Official observations provide a basis for judgments rendered in later evaluations.

Concept 13

Out-of-classroom observations also play a role in a teacher's evaluation and are documented by records of conferences and memos addressing teacher performance in areas not directly related to instruction—areas such as teacher attendance, collegiality, cooperation, and appearance.

Concept 14

Observations, both in and out of the classroom, if they are to provide valid feedback for supervision, should be data-driven, and this documentation must be shared with the teacher when it is gathered. Supervisors can develop their own methods for data collection by simply identifying their concerns and then asking themselves how they can show the teacher what they have seen and heard as the basis for these concerns.

Concept 15

Evaluations must refer back to formal observations with data collection and analysis documenting the basis for praise or criticism. Teacher's behavior receiving an unsatisfactory rating on an evaluation should have merited a warning when first observed.

Concept 16

Data collection and analysis, in order to be effective and legally defensible, must be objective, specific, and numerical. Observers should avoid using words like *many, some, a few,* and *a lot* to describe what they saw and to analyze the data collected.

Concept 17

Supervision conferences may take place before an observation but must take place after an observation. The postconference provides an opportunity to present data analysis and to work with the teacher to develop ways of eliminating identified problems.

Concept 18

Four formal models for supervising teachers include the Trait Model, the Process Model, the Instructional Objectives Model, and the Performance Objectives Model. These models differ with respect to their focuses and their procedures. Each has found some degree of acceptance as a legal and official way to supervise teachers.

Concept 19

Peer-, client-, and self-supervision are informal ways of assessing teacher performance. These methods are designated as "informal" because they are less likely to be part of a teacher's official evaluation in that the process in each of these models uses an unlicensed evaluator to assess teacher performance.

Concept 20

Nonteaching and classified positions also require supervision and evaluation on a regular basis. The Trait and Performance Objectives Models are most likely to address performance issues in these positions. Employees who are not evaluated on a regular basis cannot be held accountable for shortcomings in their performance. Attempts to discipline or dismiss them will fail if they have a property interest in their positions and have received no notice of employer concerns or help in addressing those concerns.

SUGGESTIONS FOR CLASSROOM DISCUSSION, RESEARCH, AND ACTIVITIES

1. Have students gather and compare forms and procedures for evaluating teachers in their districts and identify the models used.

2. In this chapter supervision has been described as a formative sharing of information and

insights intended to improve teacher performance during a given period of time, and evaluation as summative comments and opinions of a teacher's performance at the end of a given period of time. Have students evaluate the degree to which teachers in their districts are supervised as opposed to evaluated.

3. Have students observe a teacher and design a method for gathering objective, numerically specific data that will help the teacher to improve performance.

4. Have students discuss their own best and worst supervisory or evaluation experiences.

5. Have students research and compare procedures in their districts for supervising and evaluating tenured as opposed to nontenured teachers and classified, nonteaching staff.

CHAPTER 9: TEST QUESTIONS AND ANSWERS

1. What is remediation?

Answer: Supervision mandated by law is referred to as remediation. Supervision is a formative sharing of information and insights intended to improve teacher performance over a period of time. The process of remediation follows a formal observation visit and usually includes three basic steps:

a. the teacher must receive formal notice of the supervisor's concerns;

b. the teacher must be given time (as prescribed by law and/or contract) to improve; and

c. the teacher must be given help to improve.

2. How can it be determined whether objectionable teacher behavior is remediable or irremediable?

Answer: To determine whether objectionable teacher behavior is remediable or irremediable, three questions should be asked:

a. Were students, faculty, or schools damaged by the teacher's behavior?

b. If there was damage as the result of the teacher's conduct, could that damage have been avoided or mitigated had the teacher been warned?

c. Can the effects of the teacher's conduct be corrected?

3. Give an example of remediable teacher behavior and an example of irremediable teacher behavior.

Answer: Poor lesson planning or lesson execution are examples of teacher behaviors that are remediable. With proper warnings, instruction, modeling, and time, most teachers can learn to plan and execute effective lessons. Offensive sexual behavior is almost always irremediable in light of student immaturity, the damage and public outrage engendered, and the likelihood that such behavior would recur, and so the courts have held that sexual misconduct is a condition that cannot be remedied.

4. What is the difference between a tenured and a nontenured teacher?

Answer: Teachers with limited contracts are hired on an annual basis, have no property right to continued employment when the school year is over, and are said to be nontenured. Teachers with limited contracts can have their contracts nonrenewed at the end of any school year. In contrast, tenured teachers have continuing contracts, the expectation of reemployment from one year to the next, and a constitutional right to due process of law before their employment may be terminated. Tenured teachers can only be terminated for just cause, as delineated by state law and proven by a board of education.

5. As noted, tenured teachers have a property right to their jobs and a constitutional right to due process of law before they lose their jobs. What is due process of law?

Answer: Procedural due process requires that a teacher threatened with dismissal be accorded:

a. notice of the reason for their dismissal;

b. an opportunity to confront and cross-examine witnesses and accusers;

c. an opportunity to be represented by counsel;

d. the right to a hearing; and,

e. the right to appeal a negative decision.

Moreover, specific statutory grounds for dismissal must be actually proven by a board of education before a tenured teacher's contract can be terminated.

6. What are the rights of a nontenured teacher whose poor performance causes the school district to terminate the teacher's contract in March?

Answer: A nontenured teacher threatened with termination *before* the teacher's yearly contract has expired has a right to procedural due process because such dismissal without just cause would be a breach of contract.

7. What training do supervisors need in order to be effective in helping the teachers they supervise?

Answer: It is important to train supervisors and evaluators to observe, collect and analyze data, conference, write reports, set goals, and remediate teachers as needed.

8. Discuss ways to collect data to show a teacher that the level of questioning and classroom activity during the lesson never addresses the higher levels of Bloom's Taxonomy.

Answer: If the level of teacher questioning and classroom activity is a concern, *selective verbatim* data collection can record teacher questions and describe classroom activities, and the questions and activities can then be analyzed with respect to the level of Bloom's Taxonomy they reflect as shown in figure 9.5.

9. What are the steps involved in conducting an effective postconference with an observed teacher?

Answer: The following steps should be an integral part of postconferencing:

a. Teachers should receive the data collected and the observer's analysis of that data before the postconference. It is difficult to understand and respond intelligently to information one sees for the first time in a supervisory conference.

b. Observers should prepare questions that will help the teacher recognize and address identified concerns.

c. Observers must schedule adequate, uninterrupted time to conduct the postconference.

10. Compare the difference in focus for each of the four formal supervision models discussed in this chapter.

Answer: The Trait Model focuses on the teacher, noting the degree to which the traits of an ideal teacher appear in the observed teacher's performance. The Process Model focuses exclusively on the process of teaching, noting whether the steps in the effective teaching paradigms are present in lessons observed. The Instructional Objectives Model focuses on student achievement as the parameter for measuring teacher performance. The Performance Objectives Model focuses on teacher performance outside of the classroom, that is, the peripheral demands of the job that determine whether the teacher is a good employee, qualities such as punctuality, collegiality, and professionalism.

Chapter Ten

Staff Development

PIVOTAL CONCEPTS

This chapter presents a format and options for effective staff development. The approach to staff development presented is premised on the belief that since adult growth is a personal process rooted in individual experience and personal motivation, successful staff development creates options that allow for individualization. Eight models for teacher staff development are discussed, as well as staff development options for classified staff.

Concept 1

Schools, like all other successful organizations, have a duty to help employees grow professionally. Staff development is the process of offering employees opportunities to learn new skills and have new experiences that will enhance their personal image and professional performance.

Concept 2

Adults are self-directed, have experiences that form a knowledge base, and learn by solving problems. Adults come to every situation with an intellectual and experiential history that is unique and cannot be ignored. Growth is a personal process rooted in individual experience and personal motivation.

Concept 3

Staff development programs that provide different experiences for participants at different stages of their developments are more apt to obtain their objectives than those in which all parties engage in common activities. Parties who choose to participate in a program of staff development are more likely to find the program helpful.

Concept 4

The tendency to think of staff development only in terms of groups and majority needs undercuts what research reveals about the way adults learn, i.e., their need for individualization and personalized professional growth plans. Teacher involvement in staff development should occur during planning as well as implementation. Needs assessments are a starting point for teacher participation in planning successful programs, but teachers should also be involved in the actual selection of the speakers, formats, and environments for program components.

Concept 5

Adults, unlike students, learn best when they are directly involved in planning their learning experiences. Adults also learn best when they have choices. Thus, good staff development programs should provide options with respect to speakers, formats, activities, expectations, and goals.

Concept 6

There are eight separate models for encouraging teacher professional development: Classroom-Centered, Training, Research-Centered, Merit Recognition, School Improvement, Internal Career Ladders, External Career Ladders, and Self-Directed Plans.

Concept 7

Classroom centered staff development has the goal of making the teacher a better teacher. Professional growth objectives center on the classroom and instruction. New and veteran teachers benefit by observing colleagues, gathering data, preparing feedback, and discussing the common experience. They also learn by being observed and engaging in a discussion of the data collected during that observation.

Concept 8

Training equates with staff development in the form of the classic workshop presented by one or more speakers, experts in their fields who purport to be able to impart new skills to their audiences. Selection of workshop leaders is central to making training an effective professional growth experience and should involve comparison and evaluation of programs and presenters.

Concept 9

Improved instruction, more reflective learners, professional growth, and collegial sharing—all can result from involving teachers in classroom research. Site-based research models for professional development encourage classroom teachers to become on-site researchers exploring the effectiveness of what they do.

Concept 10

Teachers involved in school improvement initiatives grow socially, intellectually, and professionally. Socially, they have the opportunity to lead or contribute to the project and to learn from the group experience, while intellectually they are challenged to analyze problems, to identify the factors that must be addressed in solving those problems, and to develop solutions in light of these factors.

Concept 11

Career ladders, internal or external, are opportunities for growth outside of the classroom. Teachers who opt to participate in career ladder programs are recognized and rewarded for doing more than they are required to do by contract as they take on responsibilities for roles and projects that have no direct connection to their teaching assignments but do make a contribution to the educational community.

Concept 12

Merit pay plans that act as a stimulus or incentive for better teaching become a professional growth option. The Merit Pay Professional Development Model is appropriate where it is clearly observable that one employee is more productive than another and that other employees know, or can be told, what they must do to receive a merit increase in pay.

Concept 13

In self-directed professional development models, teachers are free to involve themselves in enrichment projects that may have only a tangential effect on classroom or professional performance. This plan recognizes that incorporating opportunities for individuals to pursue diverse interests will make them better professionals in the long run.

Concept 14

Just as no school employee is exempt from supervision and evaluation, so no school employee should be denied the opportunity for professional growth. In addition to job-related programs, classified and nonteaching employee groups will benefit from human resource presentations dealing with such relevant topics as employee health plans, retirement programs, workplace laws, and sexual harassment.

Concept 15

Boards of education are legally authorized and encouraged to provide staff development programs for their employees but have a collateral legal responsibility to be sure the funds expended are not misappropriated or wasted. In states that sanction collective bargaining, all staff development efforts, as terms and conditions of employment, should be duly negotiated.

SUGGESTIONS FOR CLASSROOM DISCUSSION, RESEARCH, AND ACTIVITIES

1. Have students discuss and compare state and local efforts to provide for staff development for teachers.

2. Have students take opposing positions and actively debate the pros and cons of merit pay to encourage professional growth.

3. Have students plan a needed training program for their school by comparing three presentations addressing the identified need with respect to the five elements of an effective training program presented in this chapter.

4. Have students develop their own personalized professional growth plans using one or more of the models presented in this chapter.

5. Have students design a staff development program addressing the needs of the educational assistants/aides in their schools.

CHAPTER 10: TEST QUESTIONS AND ANSWERS

1. In designing staff development for employees, human resource managers must be cognizant of how adults learn. What factors enhance adult learning?

Answer:

a. Adults enjoy planning and conducting their own learning experiences.

b. Experiences are key to self-actualization.

c. The best learning takes place when the need to know coincides with the training.

d. Adults need opportunities to apply what they have learned.

e. Adults need some independent structured options for learning.

2. What special training is needed by teachers who participate in classroom-centered staff development?

Answer: Teachers who participate in this model should be trained in clinical supervision techniques, that is, in data collection, objective analysis, and conferencing.

3. Ideally, training translates theory into practice by incorporating five distinct elements in every presentation. What are those five elements?

Answer: Effective training programs have been found to share the following elements:

a. presentation of theory;

b. modeling or demonstration;

c. practice under simulated conditions;

d. structured and open-ended feedback; and

e. coaching for application.

4. How should training programs be evaluated?

Answer: There are two prongs to this evaluation. First, was the presentation itself worthwhile and well-received. Second, did the presentation have its intended effect. Teacher surveys and interviews will measure the immediate response to training, but the true measure of training effectiveness will be determined by whether or not teachers use what they have learned, and use it effectively.

5. How can administrators support site-based research?

Answer: Administrative support for this model of staff development begins with simple encouragement and interest. Administrators who share research findings that they find interesting set the stage for teacher involvement in this staff development model. Additionally, on-site researchers should be given a forum for discussing and disseminating their findings. In-house newsletters or journals devoted to the discussion of educational research, as well as planned meetings for sharing information, give teachers the recognition and encouragement their efforts as researchers deserve.

6. Give an example of a project that would allow teachers to use the School Improvement Professional Development Model.

Answer: There are many possible answers to this question. Participation in the work of any school committee would qualify as a correct response. For example, a teacher might participate in the work of a textbook selection committee.

7. What is the difference between career ladder and merit pay plans for teacher staff development?

Answer: Teachers participating in merit pay plans are rewarded for exemplary performance in a given teaching position. Teachers participating in career ladder plans are rewarded for work they take on and complete above and beyond the work required by their given positions as teachers.

8. Give two examples of the Self-Directed Staff Development Model that illustrate the difference between it and other models discussed in this chapter.

Answer: The Self-Directed Staff Development Model allows teachers to involve themselves in enrichment projects that may have only a tangential effect on classroom or professional performance. Teachers who seek additional certification in new areas, or who wish to travel in the interest of professional growth are engaged in self-directed staff development. For example, a math teacher who chooses to learn a new foreign language is involved in professional growth, although the teacher may never choose to teach the language.

9. Give examples of staff development programs for cafeteria workers and secretaries.

Answer: Menu planning, kitchen safety, and budgeting programs address the needs of cafeteria workers. Programs dealing with office etiquette, computer and equipment use, and issues of recordkeeping and confidentiality would be growth opportunities for secretaries.

10. What are some of the legal considerations that should play a role in planning staff development programs?

Answer: Boards of education are legally authorized and encouraged to provide staff development programs for their employees. Boards have statutory authority to use district funds to cover any reasonable and necessary expense entailed. They are authorized to enter into cooperative agreements to establish and operate staff development programs for teaching, nonteaching, and classified staff. However, this authority carries with it a collateral legal responsibility to be sure the funds expended are not misappropriated or wasted. Training should be targeted to needs, and used by those trained. In states that sanction collective bargaining, all staff development efforts, as terms and conditions of employment, should be duly negotiated. In all states merit pay should be selectively awarded based on legally defensible criteria, and career ladder positions should be defined and assigned on the basis of nondiscriminatory criteria.

Chapter Eleven

Record Keeping and Reporting

PIVOTAL CONCEPTS

This chapter deals with the recording and reporting functions of human resource management. In particular, the chapter explores the tension between the privacy rights of public employees and the laws promising disclosure of public records. The importance of alerting school employees to both their legal rights and their legal responsibilities in this area is emphasized.

Concept 1

Effective human resource managers routinely gather, organize, and analyze data so that they have experiential reasons for the decisions and recommendations they make, and so they can evaluate the effectiveness of policies and procedures that are in place. There are, however, legal issues regarding the collection, maintenance, and dissemination of human resource data that are central to effective human resource management.

Concept 2

In 1974 Congress passed the federal Privacy Act ensuring the accuracy of information the federal government collects about individuals and protecting personal information from unauthorized disclosure. The states have their own privacy acts mirroring the procedures and intent of the federal Privacy Act. The seeming protection of personal privacy promised by these state and federal laws, however, is offset by the prescriptions of the federal Freedom of Information Act and similar public records laws adopted by state governments designed to give citizens access to information regarding governmental activities by requesting public records pertaining to those activities.

Concept 3

A public record is any record kept by a government agency. Since school districts are state governmental agencies, the data they routinely gather in the course of human resource management are all public records subject to disclosure under the Freedom of Information Act or State Public Records Acts.

Concept 4

There are some exceptions to the types of documentation open to citizen review. Medical records, such as physical or psychiatric exams, are generally exempt from disclosure, as are documents involving attorney/client privilege, or doctor/patient privilege. Private notes shared with no one, or purely personal communications, are also not considered public records and are exempt from disclosure.

Concept 5

As a general rule, right of access to public records is restricted only if access can be shown to endanger the safety of the record, or if access would unreasonably interfere with the operation of the agency having custody of the record. Contracts may prescribe that teachers be notified when their records are requested, that they give permission for record release, or that they have the right to review their records and contest the content. These procedural rights, however, have done little to thwart the ultimate release of public records not specifically exempted by federal or state law.

Concept 6

The courts have ruled that personnel files are subject to open records laws unless specifically exempted by law. Public record laws and the court decisions favoring disclosure seek to give members of the public information they need to address legitimate public concerns. The courts have found contracts with nondisclosure clauses contrary to public policy and unenforceable.

Concept 7

Teachers' records are not protected by the Family Educational Rights and Privacy Act that shields student records from public review. Teachers are public employees and so the public has a legitimate concern about their qualifications for the positions they hold and the caliber of their past and present performance.

Concept 8

Most public records acts, patterned after the federal Freedom of Information Act, require that public records be made available on request. The person making the request cannot be required to establish a proper purpose, or, for that matter, any purpose for a records request.

Concept 9

Public records open to disclosure include microfilm, computer disks, and videotapes, as well as written records. The person requesting access to such public records has the right to ask for copies, or to make copies of the requested records, and, in either case, they may be charged a reasonable duplication fee.

Concept 10

The requestor must ask for specific documents already in existence. State agencies, including school districts, are not required to create documents in response to requests for information, or to answer "blanket" requests for undifferentiated volumes of information.

Concept 11

State agencies are under no obligation to decipher or interpret the documents they produce upon request. The agency's sole obligation is to provide the requested record.

Concept 12

School systems should ensure that only necessary, accurate, and job-related information is included in personnel files, and that there is only one "official" personnel file in the district. One of the best ways to ensure personnel file integrity is to encourage employees to review their personnel files on a regular basis. Collective bargaining agreements may actually contain clauses requiring employee notification when items are added to the employees' files.

Concept 13

State courts may assess state agencies for reasonable attorney fees and other litigation costs reasonably incurred in any case in which a complainant has substantially prevailed in legally forcing the agency to release requested records.

Concept 14

Human resource administrators have a duty to know and understand legislation affecting any and all aspects of human resource management, and a responsibility for explaining these laws and their implications to employees. Failure to post laws where employees are likely to see them can actually cause a district to be fined.

Concept 15

Human resource managers are the link between legislated theory and administrative practice. Their role is, for the most part, ministerial. Record keeping and reporting are the two sides of the information management system, subject to law and contract prescriptions more than any other aspect of human resource management.

SUGGESTIONS FOR CLASSROOM DISCUSSION, RESEARCH, AND ACTIVITIES

1. Have students compare the privacy acts in three different states regarding the degree to which they protect teacher records from public disclosure.

2. Have students request collective bargaining agreements for teachers, a public record from public school districts other than their own, and discuss administrative willingness to comply with their requests. Were they asked to give a reason for their requests?

3. Have students compare collective bargaining agreement clauses from other districts regarding teacher records and privacy rights.

4. Have students review their own personnel files and report back on the process involved, administrative willingness to comply with that process, and the accuracy of file contents.

5. Have students visit several school districts and monitor district compliance with posting requirements. Were laws posted in one central location or in all school buildings? What is required by the laws themselves?

CHAPTER 11: TEST QUESTIONS AND ANSWERS

1. Identify each of the following personnel records as open to or exempt from disclosure: Social Security Numbers, Employee Applications, Employee Salaries, Grievance Forms, Medical Records, Leave Requests.

Answer:

a. Social Security Numbers—Exempt;

b. Employee Applications—Open;

c. Employee Salaries—Open;

d. Grievance Forms—Open;

e. Medical Records—Exempt; and

f. Leave Requests—Open.

2. What is a public record, and how do public records laws affect school district human resource management?

Answer: A public record is any record kept by a government agency. Since school districts are state governmental agencies, the data they routinely gather in the course of human resource management are all public records subject to disclosure under the Freedom of Information Act or State Public Records Acts. Physical or psychiatric exams, and documents involving attorney/client privilege, or doctor/patient privilege are among the few documents exempt from disclosure.

3. A teacher in your school has applied for a teaching position in another district. Can the hiring district request a copy of the teacher's attendance record while employed in your district?

Answer: Yes, if the district simply requests a record of the teacher's attendance, without specifically inquiring about sick days, they are simply exercising their right to review a public record. Asking specifically about sick days used, however, invites a charge of discrimination on the basis of disability.

4. A teacher in your school is accused of sexual impropriety with a student. However, the student and the student's parents refuse to bring official charges against the teacher because they fear the emotional toll the need to testify will take on the student. Without an official complaint, backed by willing witnesses, the district feels it cannot simply fire the teacher. Thus, a deal is struck. The teacher agrees to resign in a separation agreement containing a confidentiality clause made with the board. Can a newspaper reporter who has heard about this incident demand a copy of this separation agreement?

Answer: Yes. Settlement agreements are essentially contracts made by a public agency, and must be treated as public records, even if they do contain confidentiality clauses. The courts have found nondisclosure clauses contrary to public policy and unenforceable.

5. Can a principal's personal calendar be considered a public record?

Answer: Private notes shared with no one, or purely personal communications, are not considered public records and are exempt from disclosure. A principal's personal calendar may be considered a purely personal communication.

6. Can a teacher who is unhappy with the suspension without pay meted out to him for insubordination demand and receive access to all other teacher discipline records in an effort to prove that he was treated unfairly?

Answer: No. Most public records laws do not sanction random fishing expeditions. The requestor must ask for specific documents already in existence. State agencies, including school districts, are not required to create documents in response to requests for information, or to answer "blanket" requests for undifferentiated volumes of information.

7. A teacher in your district disagrees with the evaluation placed in her personnel file, and demands that it be deleted immediately. The evaluation contains a selective verbatim record of the questions she has asked during an observation, and an administrative criticism noting the low level of questioning she used throughout the class. The evaluation also criticizes her ineffective efforts to engage students and control bad behavior. How should this matter be resolved?

Answer: Employee agreement should never become an official prerequisite for including a relevant piece of information in an employee's personnel file. An honest evaluation supported by data is such a relevant piece of information. Employees who object to items or notations made in their files can be given the opportunity to request the removal of the objectionable material, and, if that request is denied, to require inclusion of an addendum giving the employee's response to the disputed entry.

8. How are public record acts enforced?

Answer: If a public agency refuses to provide the records requested, the party making the request can sue, and state courts may assess state agencies for reasonable attorney fees and other litigation costs reasonably incurred in any case in which a complainant has substantially prevailed.

9. Human resource management has an educational aspect as part of its reporting function. What are some ways of addressing this aspect of human resource management?

Answer: There are several effective approaches for addressing the educational demands of effective human resource management:

a. development and dissemination of a newsletter devoted to human resource management issues;

b. development of a series of targeted workshops addressing specific groups and legal issues, such as sexual harassment, family and medical leave, and retirement;

c. regular meetings with union leadership to monitor and discuss contract issues, such as cumbersome contract language, giving rise to grievances;

d. regular meetings with district administrators to discuss the effect of law and contract on their respective working environments; and

e. workshops for all employees regarding specific local policies and procedures connected to rights and responsibilities accorded by law and by contract, i.e., the paper trail.

10. In this chapter, referring back to a concept discussed in an earlier chapter, human resource management is described as, for the most part, ministerial. What does this mean?

Answer: Human resource managers must read, report, and apply legislated and contractual prescriptions to employee behavior in the school setting. In doing so, they are expected to simply follow law and contract already in existence, as opposed to exercising discretion in creating new laws and contracts.

About the Authors

Bernadette Marczely completed her doctoral work in educational administration at Columbia University and served as a public school teacher, principal, and district administrator before assuming her current position as a professor in the College of Education at Cleveland State University. At present, she is the director of Cleveland State's graduate program in educational supervision, a program designed to prepare and license future public school administrators.

In addition, Marczely received a law degree from Cleveland Marshall College of Law and is a licensed Ohio attorney with a practice limited to employment and labor arbitration. As an active member of the American Arbitration Association, she has been asked to render decisions on a wide variety of workplace issues in both the public and private sector.

Marczely's research centers on employment and labor law and on the application of employment and labor law to actual workplace practice. She has published extensively in these areas, particularly concerning the effect of recent court decisions interpreting existing law on the public school environment and administrative practice. This text is based on that research and is designed to familiarize future school administrators with current legal mandates affecting school management.

David Marczely completed his doctoral work in meteorology at the Pennsylvania State University and his law degree at Cleveland Marshall College of Law. David Marczely is an environmental scientist and a licensed Ohio attorney with a background in both education and business. Before coming to Ohio, Marczely was a professor at Southern Connecticut State University in the Department of Earth Science and taught both Meteorology and Earth Science.

Since receiving his law degree, Marczely has worked as an environmental compliance officer with the Environmental Design Group. This position has given Marczely the opportunity to combine both his scientific and legal interests. In addition, he is an adjunct professor at Cleveland Marshall College of Law, teaching environmental and administrative law.

Marczely is the current chair of the Northern Ohio Chapter of the Air and Waste Management Association and is its former newsletter editor. He has also published several articles dealing with environmental issues and coauthored several employment and labor law publications.

www.ingramcontent.com/pod-product-compliance
Ingram Content Group UK Ltd.
Pitfield, Milton Keynes, MK11 3LW, UK
UKHW051418150926
475561UK00005B/226

9 780810 846036